GUIDANCE
and
COUNSELLING
(For Teachers, Parents and Students)

GUIDANCE and COUNSELLING

(For Teachers, Parents and Students)

SISTER MARY VISHALA, SND

SISTERS OF NOTRE DAME
70 PALACE ROAD
BANGALORE-560 001
KARNATAKA
INDIA

S. CHAND & COMPANY LTD.

(An ISO 9001 : 2000 Company)

Ram Nagar, New Delhi - 110 055

S. CHAND & COMPANY LTD.

(An ISO 9001 : 2008 Company)

Head Office: 7361, RAM NAGAR, NEW DELHI - 110 055
Phone: 23672080-81-82, 9899107446, 9911310888
Fax: 91-11-23677446

Shop at: **schandgroup.com**; e-mail: **info@schandgroup.com**

Branches :

AHMEDABAD	: 1st Floor, Heritage, Near Gujarat Vidhyapeeth, Ashram Road, **Ahmedabad** - 380 014, Ph: 27541965, 27542369, ahmedabad@schandgroup.com
BENGALURU	: No. 6, Ahuja Chambers, 1st Cross, Kumara Krupa Road, **Bengaluru** - 560 001, Ph: 22268048, 22354008, bangalore@schandgroup.com
BHOPAL	: Bajaj Tower, Plot No. 243, Lala Lajpat Rai Colony, Raisen Road, **Bhopal** - 462 011, Ph: 4274723. bhopal@schandgroup.com
CHANDIGARH	: S.C.O. 2419-20, First Floor, Sector - 22-C (Near Aroma Hotel), **Chandigarh** -160 022, Ph: 2725443, 2725446, chandigarh@schandgroup.com
CHENNAI	: 152, Anna Salai, **Chennai** - 600 002, Ph: 28460026, 28460027, chennai@schandgroup.com
COIMBATORE	: No. 5, 30 Feet Road, Krishnasamy Nagar, Ramanathapuram, **Coimbatore** -641045, Ph: 0422-2323620 coimbatore@schandgroup.com **(Marketing Office)**
CUTTACK	: 1st Floor, Bhartia Tower, Badambadi, **Cuttack** - 753 009, Ph: 2332580; 2332581, cuttack@schandgroup.com
DEHRADUN	: 1st Floor, 20, New Road, Near Dwarka Store, **Dehradun** - 248 001, Ph: 2711101, 2710861, dehradun@schandgroup.com
GUWAHATI	: Pan Bazar, **Guwahati** - 781 001, Ph: 2738811, 2735640 guwahati@schandgroup.com
HYDERABAD	: Padma Plaza, H.No. 3-4-630, Opp. Ratna College, Narayanaguda, **Hyderabad** - 500 029, Ph: 24651135, 24744815, hyderabad@schandgroup.com
JAIPUR	: A-14, Janta Store Shopping Complex, University Marg, Bapu Nagar, **Jaipur** - 302 015, Ph: 2719126, jaipur@schandgroup.com
JALANDHAR	: Mai Hiran Gate, **Jalandhar** - 144 008, Ph: 2401630, 5000630, jalandhar@schandgroup.com
JAMMU	: 67/B, B-Block, Gandhi Nagar, **Jammu** - 180 004, (M) 09878651464 **(Marketing Office)**
KOCHI	: Kachapilly Square, Mullassery Canal Road, Ernakulam, **Kochi** - 682 011, Ph: 2378207, cochin@schandgroup.com
KOLKATA	: 285/J, Bipin Bihari Ganguli Street, **Kolkata** - 700 012, Ph: 22367459, 22373914, kolkata@schandgroup.com
LUCKNOW	: Mahabeer Market, 25 Gwynne Road, Aminabad, **Lucknow** - 226 018, Ph: 2626801, 2284815, lucknow@schandgroup.com
MUMBAI	: Blackie House, 103/5, Walchand Hirachand Marg, Opp. G.P.O., **Mumbai** - 400 001, Ph: 22690881, 22610885, mumbai@schandgroup.com
NAGPUR	: Karnal Bag, Model Mill Chowk, Umrer Road, **Nagpur** - 440 032, Ph: 2723901, 2777666 nagpur@schandgroup.com
PATNA	: 104, Citicentre Ashok, Govind Mitra Road, **Patna** - 800 004, Ph: 2300489, 2302100, patna@schandgroup.com
PUNE	: 291/1, Ganesh Gayatri Complex, 1st Floor, Somwarpeth, Near Jain Mandir, **Pune** - 411 011, Ph: 64017298, pune@schandgroup.com **(Marketing Office)**
RAIPUR	: Kailash Residency, Plot No. 4B, Bottle House Road, Shankar Nagar, **Raipur** - 492 007, Ph: 09981200834, raipur@schandgroup.com **(Marketing Office)**
RANCHI	: Flat No. 104, Sri Draupadi Smriti Apartments, East of Jaipal Singh Stadium, Neel Ratan Street, Upper Bazar, **Ranchi** - 834 001, Ph: 2208761, ranchi@schandgroup.com **(Marketing Office)**
SILIGURI	: 122, Raja Ram Mohan Roy Road, East Vivekanandapally, P.O., **Siliguri**-734001, Dist., Jalpaiguri, (W.B.) Ph. 0353-2520750 **(Marketing Office)**
VISAKHAPATNAM	: Plot No. 7, 1st Floor, Allipurám Extension, Opp. Radhakrishna Towers, Seethammadhara North Extn., **Visakhapatnam** - 530 013, (M) 09347580841, visakhapatnam@schandgroup.com **(Marketing Office)**

First Edition 2006
Reprint 2006, 2008
Second Revised Edition 2009
Reprint 2012

ISBN : 81-219-2747-1   **Code : 01A 214**

PRINTED IN INDIA
By Rajendra Ravindra Printers Pvt. Ltd., 7361, Ram Nagar, New Delhi -110 055
and published by S. Chand & Company Ltd., 7361, Ram Nagar, New Delhi -110 055.

This book is dedicated to the Youth and with a special remembrance to the Children of Beslan School Seize in Russia and the Children of Kumbakonam School Fire, Tamil Nadu.

T his book is the fruit of years of experience and reflective practice. The author has worked for many years in the establishment and development of schools in various parts of the Indian subcontinent. In seeking to offer a book that will be helpful to educators of young minds, she has drawn from real life experiences to illustrate the basic principles of applied ethics in the school situation.

Educators today do not live any longer in the predictable social context in which they were educated. Even what we thought we knew well is becoming increasingly unfamiliar. We cannot make easy assumptions about those we educate or the parents of the children who come under our influence as teachers. In fact we live in three contexts at the same time: the traditional, the modern and what is now being termed as 'the post-modern.' All three make different ethical assumptions and elicit conflicting responses from people within the same community – if one can still speak of our changing social grouping as ' communities.' Amidst the tensions of these three irreconcilable social 'words' which we confront daily, we have also to deal with the impact of globalization which uncontrollably changes the local education 'agenda' by pouring into our context problems quite alien to it. We import the best and the worst from elsewhere. Nothing stands still!

In this constantly changing social malaise, one of the most bewildering areas has been that of ethics and counselling. Our 'word', on the one hand, swings between the uncritical observance of outworn conventions and a worrying move towards fundamentalism; and, on the other hand, there is a similar uncritical liberalism that in principle believes that 'anything is O.K.' Both positions are extreme and harbour grave dangers. Educators and those who have serious concerns about the future of the community, the integrity of family life and the depth of the educational experience need all the help we can get in dealing with everyday ethical dilemmas.

Sr. Vishala's book is clear in its philosophical outlook and purpose but is based on the everyday experiences of an observant and thoughtful educational leader. They include the dilemmas of parents, teachers and students. In writing a practical help book for educators she has been especially concerned to illustrate the issues that affect the children she has dealt with, at different ages and stages of learning. She has carefully documented examples that illustrate the precepts she advocates and has been especially concerned to provide help and guidance rather than indulging in the trivia of technique or theory which so many scholarly texts indulge in. We are indebted to her.

PROFESSOR G J PILLAY
Vice-Chancellor and Rector
Liverpool Hope University
Liverpool England

ACKNOWLEDGEMENTS

A book is never the work of one single person.

I express my sincere gratitude to Sr. M. Sujita, S.N.D. Superior General and her Council Members, Rome, Italy, Sr. M. Jayanti, S.N.D. Provincial Superior, Sn. Province, India, and all my Notre Dame Sisters in India and abroad for their continuous support and encouragement in bringing out this book.

I owe my special gratitude to Prof. G. Pillay, the Vice-Chancellor of Hope University, Liverpool, England, for giving the foreword and enhancing the value of the book. His support is worth noting.

I want to offer my sincere thanks to Mr. Niel O' Brien and Mr. Francis Fanthome for their encouragement.

Many students, parents and teachers have been the inspiration to bring out this book. All the examples given in this book are the Real Life Experiences of them from their day-to-day life. The names of persons are changed for the sake of confidentiality (Both in the examples as well as in the photographs). I am grateful to all of them.

My special appreciation goes to those people who were so gracious to give their own photographs and their children's photographs. I am also grateful to the Principals of Bishop Cotton Boys School, Sophia Primary and High School, Bangalore, Notre Dame Academy, Patna, and Notre Dame School Badarpur, New Delhi, for contributing their students' photographs. Thank you for adding life and beauty to the book.

With gratitude I would like to acknowledge the great help given by Dr.Nagasubramanyam, the renowned Urosurgeon, and Dr.Padmasri Nagasubramanyam, Gynaecologist for going through the materials concerning the medical aspects and approving them. A special note of thanks to Dr. Nagasubramanyam for contributing the articles on Homosexuality and Masturbation.

I am grateful to Sister Mary Rajani, S.N.D, Sister Mary Jaya, S.N.D and Miss.Julie Lazarus for doing the proof reading. Many thanks to Mr. & Mrs. Sunny Joseph, Mrs.Veronica Stevens and Mrs. Rubianna for typing the manuscript patiently. Special thanks to Mr. Benny K. Abraham, Graphic Designer and all the other associates of S. Chand & Company Ltd. for their cooperation in bringing out this book in record time.

Some of the materials are from various sources such as notes, reference books and magazines collected during the past many years. Unfortunately

ACKNOWLEDGEMENTS

some names of the sources were not noted down for use now. Therefore, I am unable to provide an accurate and personal acknowledgement. Yet, I sincerely wish to express my gratitude to all those who have contributed towards this book.

All the possible efforts have been made to give due credit to the sources from where the materials have been taken. If inadvertantly I had forgotten to give credit then that shall be done so in the next edition of this book. Future publications will give due credit to those that are brought to the author's notice.

I gratefully acknowledge the following publishers from whom permission is sought, to use the copyrighted materials.

— **Sex and the Teenager** by Barbara Cartland. Better Yourself Books, 1972. Published by The Bombay, St.Paul Society, Bandra. ISBN.81-7108-088-X

— **Guidance and Counselling** by Dr. (Miss) Mehroo D. Bengalee. Published by Sheth Educational Publishers, Mumbai.

— **Educational Psychology** by S.K.Mangal. Published by M/S Prakash Brothers, Ludhiana.

— **Developmental Psychology**, A Lifespan Approach, Fifth edition by Elizabeth B.Hurlock. Published by Tata McGraw-Hill Publishing Company New Delhi.

Once again, my thanks goes to S. Chand & Company Ltd. for publishing this book.

It is my privilege and duty to thank my Congregation, The Sisters of Notre Dame, which had always stood for the Four Cornerstones of Education since its establishment in the year 1850, i.e.,

1. THE DIGNITY OF THE TEACHER.

2. THE WORTH OF THE INDIVIDUAL STUDENT.

3. THOROUGHNESS OF INSTRUCTIONS and

4. FAITH IN GOD.

SISTER MARY VISHALA, SND

PREFACE TO THE SECOND EDITION

The response to the 1st edition of the book was overwhelmingly encouraging from people of all walks of life–family, schools, colleges, Teacher Education Institutes and Universities.

Due to the wonderful encouragement received, I have added **six new chapters**, and a **new topic – What is Creative Thinking ?** (in Chapter 5), in the second edition of the book for the benefit of all; especially for those who are entrusted with the care of students.

The following are the new chapters :

Chapter 4   HABIT FORMATION IN CHILDREN

Chapter 7   MENTAL HYGIENE IN CHILDREN

Chapter 8   WHY DOES ONE FORGET?

Chapter 9   TRAINING IN MEMORY

Chapter 10   EXCEPTIONAL CHILDREN

Chapter 11   CHARACTER FORMATION IN CHILDREN

A new topic – WHAT IS CREATIVE THINKING ?
                has been added in Chapter 5

This book is an ideal companion for the educational system and the family in the 21st century.

Please feel free to send your comments about the book to me at the address given below.

Sr. Mary Vishala, SND
Sisters of Notre Dame
70, Palace Road
Bangalore - 560001
srvishnd@yahoo.com

PREFACE TO THE FIRST EDITION

This book is designed to help four categories of people. They are the parents, teachers, students and students of Educational Psychology and Guidance and Counselling. The book is the result of many years of working with students, parents, teachers and teacher trainees. They are the inspiration behind this book.

EVERYONE wants to have a happy and contented life both in the family front and in the professional field. Every young couple looks forward to a happy married life. All the parents want to raise their children with love and understanding and they will do everything possible for their economic and emotional security.

EVERY TEACHER likes to be called as 'The Best Teacher' whom the students love and admire till his/her death.

ALL THE STUDENTS regardless of their age and where they study, want to achieve the best results and find happiness at home, school, college and with peers.

PARENTING the children and TEACHING the students effectively and successfully are two big challenges of today.

RAISING THE ADOLESCENTS with love and understanding can be frightening and frustrating because the adolescents are quite different today from they were three decades ago. And the PARENTING has changed too.

Today's students are different and the teachers look for a peaceful and meaningful coexistence between them and the children. For this, the teachers and the parents need to understand the characteristics of children in every aspect of life at various stages of growth and development. Children also need to become aware of the changes taking place as they grow from one stage to the other. Ignorance of the changes taking place physically, intellectually, emotionally, socially, sexually, morally and spiritually can lead the youngsters and others into confusion, doubt and maladjustments.

So in order to understand them and meet some of their urgent needs, both psychological and educational, I have developed this book on 'Guidance and Counselling' for children at various stages of school. (Pre-Primary, Primary, Middle School, High School and Higher Secondary.) It is a PRACTICAL AND READER-FRIENDLY GUIDE for parents, teachers and students.

PREFACE TO THE FIRST EDITION

The book begins with what is guidance and counselling, the urgent need for guidance and counselling in the family, in the educational system and in the 21st century.

The guidance programme starts from prenatal stage and ends with a special focus on adolescence. The book contains many real life experiences of individuals, parents, teachers and students as shared by them. Many relevant illustrations are added to bring in the real life situations alive.

This book is an ideal companion for the educational system and the family in the 21st century.

Please feel free to send your comments about the book to me at the address given below.

Sr. Mary Vishala, SND
Sisters of Notre Dame
70, Palace Road
Bangalore - 560001

CONTENTS

(xvii)

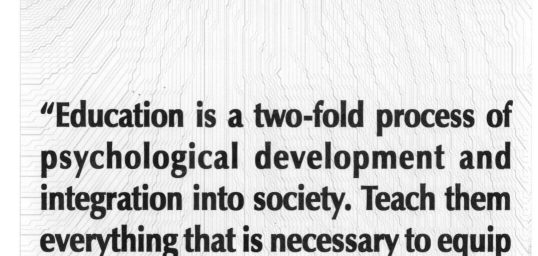

"Education is a two-fold process of psychological development and integration into society. Teach them everything that is necessary to equip them for life."

— St. Julie Billiart

CHAPTER 1

GUIDANCE AND COUNSELLING

MEANING OF GUIDANCE AND COUNSELLING

First of all let us see what guidance is, before we explain why guidance is needed. Guidance is assistance given to an individual to help him, to adjust to himself, to others and to his own peculiar environment. Guidance helps him to understand himself. It helps him in his acquaintance with the things and the world around him. Finally, it helps the person to seek harmony between his personal needs and ambitions with peculiarities of his own environment. In this way, guidance can be described as a process of assisting an individual with his adjustment problems. Thus, according to Jones, "Guidance is the help given by one person to another in making choices and adjustments and in solving problems". Skinner says "Guidance is a process of helping young persons learn to adjust to self, to others, and to circumstances".

Guidance aims to prepare an individual for his future life. It helps him to acquire essential skills, abilities and capacities for the tasks to be accomplished in future. It also helps the individual in selecting a proper future profession and role in the society and enables him to play his role successfully.

The Secondary Education Commission has given this definition "Guidance involves the difficult art of helping boys and girls to plan their own future wisely in the full light of the factors that can be mastered about themselves and about the world in which they are to live and work".

In this way, guidance has personal and social significance. It aims to help an individual in the process of his adjustment with himself and his environment. It helps him to develop his strengths and abilities, to achieve utmost personal and social efficiency. It also aims to stop wastage of human power and physical resources by helping the individuals to find their place in society.

Thus, we can say that GUIDANCE is the process of helping an individual to help himself and to develop his potentialities to the fullest by utilizing the maximum opportunities provided by the environment.

On the other hand, COUNSELLING is the service offered to the individual, who is undergoing a problem and needs professional help to overcome it. The problem keeps him disturbed, high-strung and under tension and unless solved, his development is hampered or stunted. Counselling therefore, is a more specialized service requiring training in personality development and handling exceptional groups of individuals. For example, individuals suffering from sensory handicaps like, visually handicapped, deaf and mute, speech disorders, or from physical handicaps like malfunctioning of glands or vital organs; orthopaedically handicapped ; from personal-social handicaps like, neurotics, psychotics, depressed isolates or from intellectual retardation or exceptionally high talent and so on. In other words, when the development is not normal because of certain handicaps, the individual needs help to be able to adjust to the environmental pressures and learn to overcome his handicaps or at least accept them squarely.

COUNSELLING services are therefore, required for individuals having developmental problems, because of the handicap they suffer in any area of growth like, physical, mental, moral, social and emotional, either because of hereditary factors or environmental conditions.

Generally such cases are only about five to seven percent in a population and therefore, counselling is required only for such a small number as compared to guidance which is for cent percent of individuals. Counselling involves a lot of time, for the client to unfold the problem, gain an insight into the complex situation, release the inner resources to resolve it and be convinced that he can face it and utilize his strengths to the fullest. Counselling techniques involve active listening, emphatic understanding, releasing the pent up feelings, confronting the client and so on.

Counselling, therefore is offered to only those individuals who are under serious problem and need professional help to overcome it, while guidance is needed by all at any time.

Both guidance and counselling assist the individual to know about himself, to adjust to himself, to others and the environment and thus lead the individual to become a WHOLESOME PERSON.

PHILOSOPHY OF GUIDANCE

Guidance is universal and the basic principles of the philosophy of guidance are common to all countries with a slight modification to suit the locally accepted beliefs and the specific guidance services offered. The eight principles of the philosophy of guidance are :-

  1. **The dignity of the individual is supreme.**

  2. **Each individual is unique. He or she is different from every other individual.**

3. The primary concern of guidance is the individual in his own social setting. The main aim being to help him to become a wholesome person and to gain fullest satisfaction in his life.

4. The attitudes and personal perceptions of the individual are the bases on which he acts.

5. The individual generally acts to enhance his perceived self.

6. The individual has the innate ability to learn and can be helped to make choices that will lead to self-direction, and make him consistent with the social environment.

7. The individual needs a continuous guidance process from early childhood through adulthood.

8. Each individual may, at times, need the information and personalized assistance best given by competent professional personnel.

If the above principles are accepted and followed, the guidance programme needs to be so geared that it caters to every individual in every field of activity at all times. Moreover, it needs to be provided as an individualized service, for no two individuals are identical in their development and no two guidance situations have a common base.

THE ASSUMPTIONS

The assumptions on which the principles of philosophy of guidance are based are : –

 (i) Every individual is important, unique and has talents.

(ii) Excellence is possible.

(iii) Problems may grow.

(iv) There are individual differences.

 (v) Environment provides innumerable opportunities.

THE GOALS TO ACHIEVE IN GUIDANCE

At present, guidance has taken an unprecedented lead over all the other helping professions, for it empowers an individual to charter his life successfully, inspite of all odds.

THE MAIN GOALS ARE

1. **Exploring The Self :** The basic aim is to help an individual increase his understanding and acceptance of self ; his physical development, his intelligence, aptitudes, interests, personality traits, attitudes and values, his achievements in scholastic and other spheres, his aspirations and life-style preferences and above all his here-and-now needs which keep him highly motivated to behave positively or otherwise.

2. Determining Values : The second aim is to help an individual recognize the importance of values, explore different sets of values, determine personal values and examine them in relation to the norms of society and their importance in planning for success in life.

3. Setting Goals : This aim is to help an individual set goals for himself and relate these to the values determined by him so that he recognizes the importance of long-range planning.

4. Explore the World of Work : The aim here is to help the individual explore the World of Work in relation to his self-exploration, his value system and goals that he has set for himself to achieve success in life.

5. Improving Efficiency : The individual is helped to learn about factors which contribute to increase effectiveness and efficiency and to improve his study habits.

6. Building Relationship : The aim is to help the individual to be aware of his relationship with others and to note that it is a reflection of his own feelings about himself.

7. Accepting Responsibility for the Future : The individual is helped to develop skills in social and personal forecasting, acquire attitudes and skills necessary for mastering the future.

To sum up, guidance empowers him to be an integrated individual, actualizing his potential to the fullest.

WHY GUIDANCE ?

Guidance is needed at every stage of development right from the beginning of life till the end. Everyone needs guidance at one time or the other. If properly guided, every individual will be satisfied in life.

The comprehensive view of the need for guidance in an individual's life can be divided into different stages of development.

THE STAGES OF DEVELOPMENT

According to Biehler, the five definite stages of development from the guidance point of view are :

1. Stage of Growth upto 13 years : This stage is regarded as the stage of fantasy. The individual has rapid physical and mental development and participates in all types of activities irrespective of whether it suits his abilities, temperament or not. He fantasises himself in future roles without considering whether he can actually accomplish them. He has still not developed his value system and a definite plan of action to forge ahead. The need for guidance at this stage is most important in the area of development and adjustment. If for any reason, he feels thwarted or strangulated, it would permanently damage his personality, e.g., if parental attitudes are dominant or overprotective ; or there is tremendous sibling jealousy, or there is unhealthy antagonistic environment at school. Guidance is also needed in the area of educational and professional development.

2. **Stage of Exploration :** This is the second stage of development from the age of 13 to 25 and is called the tentative stage. By 13, the individual begins to show specialization as special abilities or aptitudes come into prominence. From the world of fantasy, he begins to settle down to a certain plan of action or shows consistency in his participation of activities, not randomly selected or visualizes an educational course which will lead him to his vocational choice and so on. As mentioned, he begins to explore all opportunities coming his way and makes a choice, not out of sheer pleasure or fancy but out of careful considerations of what is possible for him or good for him. Guidance is needed most in the adjustment area, as the individual enters adolescence and finds himself lost with the world around him. Most of the work of a guidance counsellor is concentrated at this stage of development. If the individual is properly guided at this stage, his further development will be facilitated.

3. **Stage of Establishment:** This is the third stage in the development progress between the age group of 25 and 40 years, and it is called the realistic stage. By now, the individual is in a career and has completed formal training and education. He has to gain vocational development, adjustment and maturity. Guidance may be required, if the individual finds that his inter-personal relationship is not in order and is not able to get along with his colleagues or his boss. If he has developed sensitiveness to the miseries of the people around him and desires to do some civic or community service to the disturbed or the handicapped, he may ask guidance in the area and plan his time and energy to gain maximum satisfaction.

4. **Stage of Maintenance :** The fourth stage is referred to as a stage of stability, between ages of 40 and 65. He has by now accomplished all what he needs to and has almost come to the stage of retirement. The guidance that he needs, at this stage is with regard to economic matters and leisure time. If he is dependent on his children, at this stage, he normally intends passing his time in religious activities and projects connected with religious institutions.

5. **Stage of Decline :** This is the fifth stage, around the age of 65 to 75, when the adjustments become the most. Unless the individual has had a full, contented life, this period becomes one of trials and tribulations. The greatest need is to help the individual to feel that he is wanted, that he is still useful and that his family members care for him. Also gradually, he needs to be prepared to face death and whatever his ailments be, he has to learn to bear them with courage and cheerfulness till the very end.

Thus, we see that at each stage of development, guidance is required and is necessarily sought and if given systematically and scientifically it will help to make the individual fully satisfied and life worth living.

THE NEED ESTABLISHED BY KOTHARI COMMISSION [1964-1966]

The Kothari Commission Report recommended that guidance and counselling should be regarded as an integral part of education meant for students and aimed at assisting the individual to make adjustments and decisions from time to time. The summary of recommendations are :

i) **Guidance at the Primary Stage :** Guidance should begin from the lowest class in the primary school and in view of the large numbers of schools involved, the programme may be introduced through simple measures, such as (a) familiarizing teachers under training with diagnostic testing and the problem of individual differences (b) organizing in-service courses for primary teachers (c) production of occupational literature and (d) helping pupils and parents in the choice of further education.

ii) **Guidance at the Secondary Stage :** Guidance at the secondary stage helps in identifying and developing of abilities and interests of adolescent pupils. The ultimate objective should be to introduce adequate guidance services in all secondary schools with a trained counsellor in charge of the programme. But in view of the limited financial and personnel resources, a short range programme should be adopted for the next 20 years consisting of :

(a) A minimum guidance programme for all secondary schools through a visiting school counsellor for a group of 10 schools assisted by the school teachers in the simpler guidance functions. (b) Comprehensive guidance programme in selected schools, one in each district, to serve as models, and (c) Provision of necessary supervisory staff in the State Bureaus of Guidance.

iii) **All Secondary School Teachers** should be introduced to guidance concepts through pre-or in-service training. The training colleges would be suitably staffed for the purpose.

iv) **General :** Arrangements should be made for the professional training of guidance workers by the State Bureaus of Guidance and Training Colleges. Advanced training should be organized at the national level.

v) **Ancillary Programmes** should include the production of guidance literature and materials and research into problems of guidance in the Indian situation.

Thus, it is very clear that the Education Commission has rightly emphasised on guidance services at all levels of education and has suggested suitable methods for implementing the same.

GUIDANCE IN MODERN SOCIETY

Guidance is needed by everyone. Today's world is highly complex in every sphere of life. To begin with, we have the family which has changed its many traditions, customs, beliefs, values and attitudes. Then, the school and the modern society in the 21st century. The individual is influenced by his family, his educational environment and by the society. Therefore, it is good to have a look into these three areas and the changes which have taken place in them.

THE FAMILY

Some features of the family in the 21st Century:

- break up of the Joint Family System

Fig. 1.1. Children spending quality time with their parents and grandparents

- nuclear family
- single parent
- divorced parents
- separated parents
- working parents (both the parents).
- changes in the old traditions, customs and family values which were healthy for the emotional security and development of children.

Fig. 1.2. Responsible fathers spend time talking to their kids

- the norm of one child or maximum two children.
- preference for a male child and neglecting the girl child to the extent of killing her through abortion.
- the position of the child in the family.
- the economic status of the family.
- certain beliefs and superstitions.
- inter-religious and inter-caste marriages.

As the world has shrunk, so has the family. With the breaking up of the joint family system, nuclear families have increased. The traditional old system was a large family or a joint family, while if we look into our family set up today, we find that majority of them are a single unit with one child or maximum two children, the son is separated from the parents and established on his own. A loneliness pervades in their lives.

The break up of the joint family system has resulted in two major economic problems for the well-being of the family.

The first one being the lowering of the economic standards and duplicating of expenses. The acute housing problem and the slum-dwellings could have been eased, if the practice of the joint family continued.

Too many people, too few houses. More families mean the need for more houses. From large sprawling bungalows with plenty of space for all, our dwelling places have been reduced to smart but small flats where we lead our cramped lives, and among the lower middle and lower classes, the only option is to live in slums, with little space, little privacy and almost no freedom.

Space, we all know, pervades the universe. Too much or too less can destroy inherent balances and harmonies. In families, too much of space - physical and emotional – can translate into emotional detachment. It doesn't help the children at all and too less space means over-protectiveness and claustrophobia. The second is the physical, psychological, emotional and social insecurity of the members of the family. In the joint family, there is a strong physical, emotional and social support system. The breakup of the joint family system has caused considerable harm from the psychological point of view. There is a

Fig. 1.3. Maddening crowds of the cities

lot of genuine love and affection among the children growing under one roof. There is a tremendous scope for sharing everything, from food to clothing, from study to play, from secrets to suggestions. Most of the social virtues of cooperation, team spirit, making sacrifices, coordination and so on can be imbibed without any conscious effort on the part of the individual. Even if there is a loss of a parent,

there is some elderly person in the family, who takes up the role and does not let the individual suffer. Having grown in a joint-family set up, the individual's transition from family to school and later to the society at large is smooth and without friction, for he has learnt the basic lessons of give and take, of cooperation and competition, and of living together.

There may be a few disadvantages of the joint family system but from the guidance point of view, in a country like ours, where the resources are limited, population is uncontrollable, unemployment exists even among the educated, the joint family system was a blessing in disguise by all counts.

Let us now look into our family today, where both parents are working. In order to

Fig. 1.4. Close knit – joint family

maintain a certain standard and provide basic amenities to the members of the family, both the parents, the father and the mother need to earn. This means that both of them are out of the house, eight to ten hours of the day and return only for meals at night and for rest. Such a home is not a congenial environment for children to grow in, for it can be compared to a boarding house where people merely gather for food and rest, and exchange a few greetings without influencing one another. A home for children should provide acceptance, warmth, loving care, affection and full time attention for their well-being. By providing the physical amenities, many a parents feel that their responsibility is over. What children need, especially in the early years of development, is psychological and emotional support, a feeling of being secure and protected and having the mother by their side.

The fact remains that because, the mother goes out to earn, she keeps a servant to do the household work, sends clothes to laundry for washing, get clothes tailored or buy readymade clothes, arranges a tutor for the children, gets food from outside, and if she wishes she cooks, stores food in refrigerator and so on.

Little Neeta (name changed) was a perfect baby in everyway. But her academic performance from Class IV onwards started declining and her weight kept on increasing rapidly. When she reached Class VI she had to be given a bigger chair since the regular chairs meant for her classmates was not enough. Her poor performance in academics and her obesity had already made her feel quite awkward among her own classmates. By the time she reached high school she had to be referred to the doctors and psychiatrist for help. Later what became clear in Neeta's case was that she was always left with a housemaid at home while her parents were away till very late at night. The child hardly saw her parents. Even on holidays the parents spent time holidaying or at late night clubs. So the housemaid met all her needs by supplying chocolates or ice-cream from the refrigerator. Thus the only companions for Neeta were her housemaid and a refrigerator with eatables. Neeta's mother was rather late to realize that she had neglected her daughter.

Thus, all the services needed at home, like cooking, cleaning, washing, stitching, tutoring the child, which could be done systematically, efficiently and intelligently by the lady of the home for the physical and mental health of the members of the family are left entirely to hired labour. More than this the danger is that when the mother is away, the children are left without any control and they loiter around or spend time at the corner of the street or remain at a friend's place and they spend their time uselessly. They may also fall prey to anti-social elements and before anything can be done to improve their behaviour, they may become delinquents and chronic drug addicts.

Once a teenager who was caught for breaking some equipment in the school, revealed to me while having a guidance session how he missed his father who was separated from his mother.

Therefore, not only the small children, even the grown-up children desire to have their parents close by and to attend to their needs.

These days child abuse is common and it may be happening among one's own relatives.

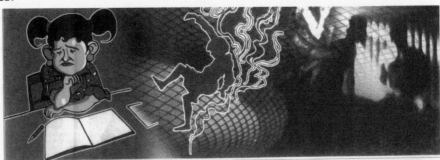

Home is where the abuse is..

Cases of girl children sexually abused by close family members are often hushed up due to various factors, learns **Tirtho Banerjee.**

Anjali has never been like this before. The little nine-year-old girl shuns the company of her friends. She has been bed-wetting for the last few weeks. What's more, her teacher informed her parents that she has not been doing her lessons properly.

Courtesy : Deccan Herald, Friday, September 17, 2004

Here is a wise piece of advice for parents who have daughters. Please do not let them stay away in your friend's or relative's house if you are not with them. There are some parents who send their small daughters to their friend's and relative's house in far away places during holidays. These open opportunities for child abuse and cause permanent damage to the child and her future.

Fig. 1.5. A totally confused and traumatised little girl

Perhaps, the demand for more social-welfare agencies, child-guidance clinics, psychologists and counsellors is increasing because of this growing menace of social evils which were unheard of three decades ago in our Indian society.

When both the parents are out the whole day, there is hardly any time to spend with the child to provide guidance in the academic and personal problems. They can't provide academic guidance or help them in sorting out their learning problems. Even in the choice of subjects, the selection is so wide that they themselves are ignorant of the possibilities and cannot venture to re-educate themselves. The potential of their own children is also not properly explored by them.

It is also seen that a working mother becomes rather independent and less respectful to her husband and these may lead to constant quarrels and disagreements. She is too tired after the day's work, to attend to the household chores, as well as the demands of her family. As a result, each member seeks satisfaction and happiness outside the home rather than at home. If at all they gather together, it would be for meals, for that also they may keep different timings lest they clash.

"MY MOM REALLY LIKES WORK," says Christine. If both the parents have to spend a lot of time on work, particularly at evenings or weekends when the child is around, then the child may form the conclusion, **"MOM WOULD RATHER WORK THAN BE WITH ME".**

Children are not able to comprehend why parents must have other pre-occupations than them. The feeling of the child is likely to be that if mom and dad liked me they would want to be with me.

Thus, the absence of the working mother, from home has really resulted in grave consequences and even in the most progressive countries, the women are questioning the wisdom of earning and rearing children simultaneously or in other words, playing the double role of a mother and an employee. If at all, the mother has to earn because of economic necessity, there are ways and means of earning at home and subsidizing the income. The psychological need to work also can be fulfilled and she may engage herself in some productive work in her spare time. Guidance is needed at a young age to prepare her for such careers which she can continue even after marriage and during child rearing period.

It is important to explain to your children, when you are not able to spend much time with them because of work commitments. Tell them that you too are disappointed. Give a simple factual explanation of the work situation. Focus on how disappointing it is for you both for not being able to spend time together. Give the children something to look forward to - but be realistic. Do not promise to take them for an outing next Saturday unless you are very sure that the work pressure will be over by then. While you are waiting for the treat, throw into the conversation: "I'm really looking forward to next Saturday, when we are going for an outing together."

Many couples have adopted the norm of one child. The only one child formula has caused certain problems for the child itself such as selfishness or not able to cope up with other children because of lack of sharing and generosity between siblings.

Such an only child may also have a problem of attention seeking. Like the eight-year-old Susan who was extremely irritating to her teachers, was a sort of little girl who always seemed to be asking for unnecessary additional help. One teacher quoted a particularly irritating habit while writing in her exercise book, on reaching the end of the page, she would go and ask the teacher; "Shall I take a new page?" The teachers were sympathetic towards her, thinking that her behaviour could be a communication that she needed attention. Such attention seeking behaviour pattern continued. What emerged later was that Susan was the only child of her parents. Both the parents had busy careers involving not only long hours, but also a good deal of social entertaining. Susan grew up feeling jealous of her parents' relationship. They were always going out together. To her it felt that they would rather have each other than her. They took a greater pleasure in each other's company than in hers.

In families where there is more than one child, the sibling rivalry is a natural phenomenon. In some cases, there will be such intense sibling rivalry and jealousy if the older child is not prepared well before the arrival of the new member in the family. If the parents are sensitive to the feelings of existing children and respond with understanding, rivalry may be kept to a minimum.

Neglecting or rejecting the female child and preferring a male child is common in India. This has caused enormous harm to the girls. Many girls suffer rejection in their early childhood and become depressed when they are already in their teens. Girls are not given proper education, in some cases. Therefore, guidance is needed for the parents to accept their female children and to give equal opportunities for them. The girls need guidance in order to cope up with the rejection and for better adjustment in life as a worthwhile member of the family and society.

Another drawback today is that there are no more hereditary occupations into which the child can be absorbed. Even the skilled craftsmen prefer their children to pursue higher academic education at the cost of losing the traditional skills with a hope that they would enter white-collar jobs. Even the highly qualified professionals' children cannot enter their practice because of the stiff competition they have to face for professional courses. The business houses' children too find it difficult to enter their own business. With trade unions, only the qualified are recruited and that too through the employment exchange. Hence, the problems have increased even of placement of their children and proper guidance is needed to solve them.

If we look into our 21st century families, we find that many of the inter-religious and inter-caste marriages ending in deep troubles and children becoming the victims. Therefore, proper guidance is a must before and after such marriages, so that the break up of the marriages may be kept to minimum.

The study of an Indian family will reveal that children are losing respect for their parents and elders and are becoming far too bold and indisciplined. Many have no hold on their religious faith, or have no common prayers. The good old saying that, "A family which prays together, stands together" has much value these days. There is too much of laxity and permissiveness and on occasion, they threaten the parents to dire consequences, if they are punished. The value system is undergoing a rapid change and the family norms are regarded as things to talk about and not practice.

THOUGHTS FOR REFLECTION

• Are you the parents who give good examples to your children?

• How do you live out the family values like love and affection, respect for each other, acceptance and appreciation, caring, self-sacrifice, forgiveness and generosity?

• Do you respect each child as a unique gift of God?

• Do you give equal rights and education to your female children? Or do you try to eliminate the female child through abortion?

• Do you discipline your children properly?

• Do you spend sometime with your children?

• Do you pray together with your children? Do you enjoy taking meals with your family?

Remember each and every life has to be respected. We have no right to destroy or take away another person's life. *A family that prays together, eats together, stays together.* Children don't need perfect parents, they need parents who are good enough.

After having a brief look into our modern family system, we can with conviction conclude that there is an increasing need for guidance in all the areas of development like educational, vocational, personal, social and religious fields. Guidance is required not only for the children but also for their parents, for the entire family environment needs to be studied in the correct perspective to render help.

THE SCHOOL

Guidance is most important while the child is at school and is undergoing rapid development; physical, mental, moral, social and personal. Though girls develop and mature earlier than the boys, by the age of 16, boys have attained physical and mental maturity and have developed a pattern of interests and personality traits which may remain almost permanent with them. By now they have finished their general education and they are on their onward journey for professional and technical training. Therefore, it is an established fact that guidance has to be given at school so that children can pursue their higher studies according to their interest and aptitude, which would help in their future development and self-actualization.

A CLOSER VIEW AT THE EDUCATIONAL SYSTEM IN THE 21ST CENTURY:

- schools and colleges with very high standard providing high quality modern facilities, including human resources and material resources.
- schools and colleges with high standard.
- schools and colleges with average standard.
- schools and colleges without any standard and any facilities.
- most of the remote villages without any schools.
- educational institutions which charge exorbitant fees.
- lack of quality teachers.
- poor methods of teaching.
- mass approach in classroom.
- commercialization of education.
- In many cases higher education and professional courses are bought by money and power rather than on merit of the students.
- Too much pressure for the parents and for the students.

With the problem of over-population and crowded cities most of the existing schools can't provide a healthy atmosphere for the students. The infrastructure and resources for the schools are very limited according to the ever increasing number of students. Most of the old well established schools' classrooms were made to accommodate maximum 20 or 30 children. But now those classrooms are bulging beyond capacity and may be accommodating 55 to 60 children. Not to mention the other facilities, like sanitation, drinking water and a small playground. In such overcrowded classrooms, the pupils spend six to seven hours, sitting up on stiff chairs or benches at times and in some cases without proper lighting and ventilation too. The school curriculum with many subjects, which are not according to their choice, bring in a lack of interest for learning along with uninteresting methods of teaching by the teachers. Naturally, there would be restlessness and undesirable behaviour on the part of the children. There is no homogeneity among pupils in a class and therefore, mass instruction becomes too easy for the intelligent and too difficult for the slow learner. Problems crop up when indifference is shown by these two extreme groups and the class as a whole may suffer with regard to the rate of exposition or the expected accomplishment. Large classes are difficult to control and more so when there is not sufficient place for the free movement of the teacher from one end of the classroom to the other. Today's teachers have lost their talent and what was earlier the 'Guru-Shishya relationship. The reverence and respect, of the teacher has been totally reversed. It may be a good question to ask, have today's teachers become more commercial minded than service minded? Genuine dedication and the zeal of the teachers like the past to care for the weak students and to help in the overall development of all the pupils are rarely seen now. Teachers with missionary zeal and real mastery of their subjects are rarely seen. The educational courses have also severed from the preparation of specific job requirements so that after completion the pupils still find themselves at square one, from where they began and gained employment. So the pupils do not see the value of education when they find that it is not going to lead them to a definite career. They just drift, get restless and perhaps, drop out of the educational programme out of sheer disgust. In such a situation, guidance is needed to make them realize where to halt in general academic education and when to start technical vocational training for taking care of their future life.

These days parents will do anything in order to give good education to their children and put them in such schools which may not suit the pocket of the father. As a result the mother also may start working in order to bring additional income. This can again have a negative effect on the family as the mother finds no time to care for her husband and children.

Parents need guidance in the selection and choice of schools that have a good curriculum and are according to their budget. The modern aim of education are five fold :

(1) Lifelong learning, (2) Early productivity, (3) Quick money, (4) Sensitivity to the socio-economic environment and (5) Self-actualisation. In order to achieve these aims, a well organized guidance programme is needed to make the individual aware that what he learns today will be outdated tomorrow, therefore he needs to be open to the new learning and be a perpetual learner. Early productivity and quick money making are the needs of the day. He has to plunge in vocational preparation immediately after secondary school stage and enter the employment market by the age of 18, so that he gets full 40 years of work life. In due time he'll become an expert in his field early in life and his productivity will increase and be a self-fulfilled person for himself and for others. He has to develop sensitivity for the down-trodden, the destitute, the elderly and the handicapped. This is very much needed in our own country where there is illiteracy, poverty, caste system and religious taboos, which separate human beings from their own fellowmen. Once he has become fully developed and made use of all the opportunities available for him to excel himself in life and to serve his family and build a better society, we can say that he has achieved self-actualisation in his life.

Thus in 21st century, the need for guidance is felt much more in the educational institutions, for the authorities are aware that their efforts will yield results only if proper guidance and service is provided.

THE 21ST CENTURY SOCIETY

The following are some of the characteristics of 21st century society :

- **changes in the family system**
- **challenges of permissive society**
- **gap between the rich and the poor**
- **poverty and unemployment**
- **unequal opportunities**
- **corruption in various areas of life**
- **decline of the value system**
- **caste system**
- **globalization and advanced science and technology in every sphere of life.**

Let us focus our attention on the social and cultural, scientific and technological milieu in which our children are growing and developing.

Fig. 1.6. Young boys and girls of 21st century is permissive society, enjoying 'drinks and dance' in the discotheques

The break-up of the joint-family system, the changes in the traditions and value system of family life and most of the families being a single unit are some of the main features of the modern family. The 21st century is a permissive society, where the boys and girls move freely as compared to the older system where girls lived under the protective care of the parents at home. Even in the diet, there has been a drastic change. Girls rarely consumed tea or coffee, but now every pub and cafe are filled with freely moving girls and boys. Girls and boys move out for dance, music and other entertainments and they participate in these freely which were

Fig. 1.7. Children from the under privileged strata of the Indian Society

not done earlier. The permissive society in the 21st century has many adverse effects on the life of youth today. Thus proper guidance is needed without delay.

Over-population, illiteracy, child labour and unemployment causing frustration among the educated and the uneducated are a big burden and suffering in the modern society. The gap between the rich and the poor is increasing instead of lessening and the poorer people feel the injustice of not being sufficiently cared for or protected by the Government. It is noticed that all around majority of people live in dire poverty and only a very small number are really living in luxury. But the unfortunate part is that under the towering sky-scrapers are the thousands of slum-dwellers, who do not even have a decent roof above them. The stark difference hurts the eye and intolerable for the sufferer. Even the professionals and highly skilled technicians find it difficult to have two ends meet and are drifting from upper-middle class status to middle and those engaged in white-collared jobs are sliding to lower middle class. Obviously, there is discontentment pervading in the society for whether educated or otherwise, each individual has to struggle hard for the basic necessities of food, clothing and shelter which are becoming scarce, due to the explosion of population. Whatever economic policies are tried or man-power planning done or taxation visualized, the efforts of the government are counter balanced by the ever-growing illiterate population which seems a threatening force. Also a few calculating individuals who use counter intelligence to waive the heavy taxation on their profits harm national interests. It is a pity that we have still not been able to develop in our people the spirit of nationalism which would make them duty-conscious to pay their taxes and invest in the National Schemes and projects for rapid development of technology which could raise the masses from abject poverty.

When children see around them different standards of living or are themselves suffering from the lack of daily bread, shelter and unemployment, they grow bitter and develop a hardened way of dealing with those who are around them. If guidance is not given at the correct time, they may grow so offensive that they may harm their own development.

The other fact to be considered is that the individual does not have an equal opportunity in the society. Though equality is accepted by the democratic socialistic set-up of our country, yet in reality there are innumerable imbalances and prejudices in all areas. For example, the rich can afford to send their children to private schools which charge exorbitant fees and provide varied curricular and co-curricular activities for an allround development of the child as well as for rigorous training in a certain talent in which the child excels. While on the other hand, a poor parent sends his child to a Municipal School or a grant-in-aid school which has limited number of academic activities, may be because of the numbers to cater to or shift system.

Another typical injustice of unequal opportunities is noticed in the work situation. Though the government, through legislation has provided for the recruitment into commercial, industrial and goverment concerns through employment exchanges and state selection boards, every individual is aware of the fact that the employer will have his own person and if it is a private industry, will have his own nominee as the executive or the manager. This creates a lot of heart-burning for those individuals who have high qualifications and have to work as subordinates under bosses who have neither the calibre nor qualification to man the seat.

The caste system and the communal feelings are so deeply ingrained in our Indian culture that the unequal opportunities and other discriminations are also seen in other areas of development as well. At every step the individual faces several odds and needs to have built-in resources to face reality and weigh facts of life to surmount them and not crumble under their burden. Guidance alone can help him to glide over the difficult periods.

Fig. 1.8. Adults indulged in corruptions such as 'bribery'.

Another cause for concern and anxiety is the declining of value system in our 21st century. Dishonesty and corrupt practices are the ways of life for many. The character is no more a strength but money is considered as the power of character now. The wealthy nations dictate the poor and undeveloped nations. Those, who seem to have made a success in life have been able to do so by corrupt practices. A sincere, honest individual can never reach the peak of his powers or the highest position unless he has political connections. The deep roots of corruption have seeped into the temples of learning and those who can afford can buy a seat in the best of professional colleges get the best degree with least effort. Children see around them all such corrupt practices and feel despondent and discouraged to put in hard work and sincere effort. They learn very soon how to get quick money and how to indulge in anti-social or unproductive activities at the cost of hampering the economy of the country. Those who refuse to fall in line with the corrupt ways, feel frustrated and disillusioned and take to drugs, alcohol or anything to keep them away from the unbearable situations. We know what is happening in our university campuses and why young people are revolting. Instead of falling apart, guidance helps the individual to face the reality and plays a vital role in improving the state of things. Thus guidance certainly will help individuals as well as the society.

In the modern society, right from the changes in the family background to the challenges of permissive society, there are innumerable situations which need immediate help from guidance counsellors. If guidance is not provided, the individual may drift from one stage to another without any purpose and lead an aimless life. He may make his life full of drudgery and dissatisfaction and may permeate the same feeling to others around him. Not only will he make himself unhappy but also everybody else who comes in his contact. It is very important to realize that in spite of the changing times and new challenges before the individual, planning his life ahead helps him to go forward. Therefore, he must plan. The better the planning, the greater the chances of him making a success of his life.

Technology rules the world. It has thrown up many labour-saving devices. But more importantly, it has shrunk distances and made modes of travel and communication easy. So much so, that many Indian companies now serve as an extension of offices in the U.S. What does this mean for the family life? Since in most cases, we have to match our work time with the West, working in shifts has become increasingly common. If one parent is on a normal 9 to 5 shift, the other works all night. When do they get to see each other? When do the children see them? Latch-key children are a new age phenomenon–children who return from school and have to fend for themselves because both parents are at work. No doubt, when both husband and wife work, it means more money at the disposal of the family. But it also means a highly stressed-out family with little or no time for relaxation.

The workplace has also given women a new place in society. It has given them opportunities to prove themselves and excel in fields. With women increasingly becoming independent, ego hassles are now almost common. Quarrels and conflicts become a norm and once more, it's the children who suffer.

'Everyone knows all the questions, but no one knows the answers,' is what T.S. Elliot once said about the 20th century. As we are in the 21st century, there are a million more questions that people have about nuclear arms, population explosion, globalization, mechanization, instable politics, tottering economics, religious ferment, environment, unilateral war against terrorism and the list goes on.

With these questions come doubts, uncertainties and fears. Without proper guidance, life can become nasty, brutish and short.

In such a scenario, it is quite obvious that the educational system carries a massive responsibility.

Mr. B. G. Pitre has stressed on the importance of global attitudes to be effective teachers. He has emphasized on BE, DO and TELL to be excellent role models for our students. According to him, the methods of teaching that revolve around Information, Instruction and Inspiration were the most effective ways to educate our children.

The changes in the 21st century have already begun - the doubling of the human

Fig. 1.9. Teacher assisting a student

life span, blurring of roles between humans and machines, genetic engineering, cloning, environmental hazards, terrorism, AIDS, decline the values. But all of us have a role which is more important than any super computer because only teachers can touch young human beings with moral values and with feeling and care.

Therefore, educational guidance must form an integral part of education today.

WHAT IS EDUCATIONAL GUIDANCE ?

Educational Guidance can be defined as the help given to an individual to help himself to interact with conditions, processes and stimuli provided by the educational environment to actualize his potential to the fullest - whatever problems arise out of the individual's interaction with the educational environment, say, innumerable educational courses to select from, teacher-pupil relationships, inability to cope up with certain subjects and so on. When help is sought from the counsellor pertaining to individual's educational development and when the counsellor would have to move to the educational institutions for identifying the problem, we could refer to it as educational guidance.

EDUCATIONAL PROBLEMS

There are innumerable problems related to the pupil's physical and mental disabilities or to his interaction with others in the educational environment like the teachers, classmates, undue pressures and so on.

• Disinterest in studies. The pupils hate to do any school work, and reluctantly come to school. They look forward to holidays, under the slightest pretext take holidays and pretend to be ill.

• Sudden drop in scholastic performance without any apparent cause. He just cannot cope with studies.

• Fails in certain subjects consistently even with special coaching.

• Under-achievers in the schools, who with high potential make a low grade due to disinterest in school work and therefore, put in the least effort.

• Over achievers, who with limited potential exert a lot to make the grade with the help of tutors for each subject.

• Slow learners, pupils who really are unusually slow in their overall pick up.

• Then we have the scholastically backward pupil, a child who is two years older than the average age for the class and has already repeated once or twice in the same class. These pupils may sometimes be a nuisance to the teachers as they show their presence in the class by noise and anti-social activities. Scholastic backwardness could be due to a variety of causes. There may be a stray case of a mentally retarded child in the class.

• There may be another group of pupils found in a school who have no goals in life, no ambition to motivate them to study. There are certain educational problems which spring from the interaction of the pupil with the teacher and of the pupils with one another in the class. For example, if he finds that the teacher does not know his subject well and the teacher doesn't like him, the pupil will make no progress during that year and may create a number of problems thereafter. For example, a particular student broke the science apparatus in the lab because he hated the teacher who taught science.

• Partiality shown by the teacher, injustice as seen by the pupil, is no longer tolerated today.

• The other psychological and behavioural problems also interfere with scholastic performance.

• What is the best method to teach and develop positive relationship are also areas of educational guidance. The importance of such guidance can be seen more seriously when one realizes that during the school career, the individual has the maximum allround development from age six to sixteen in all aspects – physical, mental, social, personal, moral and religious and therefore, if he gets entangled in any problem, his total development would be hampered almost permanently.

VARIOUS STAGES OF EDUCATIONAL GUIDANCE

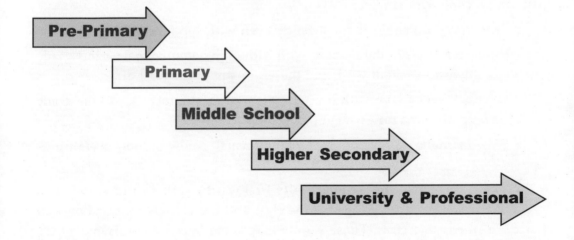

- Pre-Primary
- Primary
- Middle School
- Higher Secondary
- University & Professional

Educational guidance is required, at every stage of education, namely pre-primary, primary, middle school, high school, higher secondary, university and professional.

But this book deals with only upto higher secondary stage. The special feature of this book is that the guidance starts with Pre-natal stage and concludes it with a special focus on adolescents.

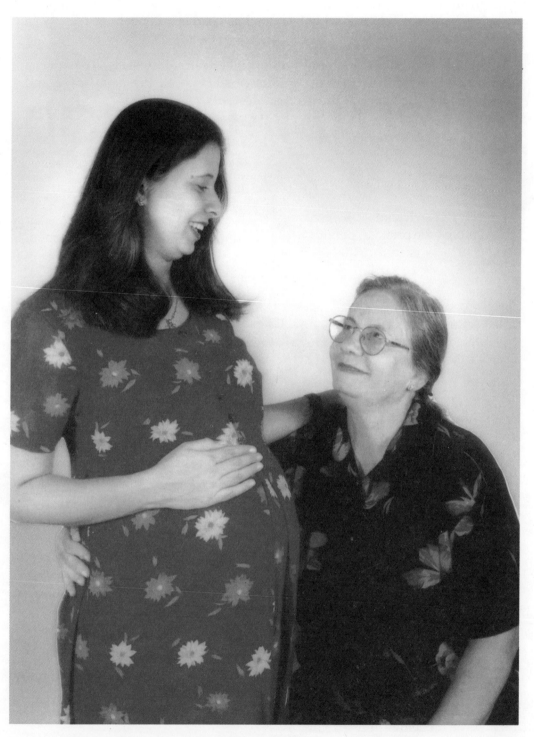

Fig. 2.1. The arrival of a baby is often referred to as a "Gift from God"

CHAPTER 2

PRENATAL PERIOD

Early research studies in developmental psychology, guidance and counselling ignored the prenatal period. It was only in the mid 1940's that developmental psychologists turned their attention to the prenatal period.

MEANING OF PRENATAL DEVELOPMENT AND ITS SPECIAL FEATURES

It was recognized that knowing what happened before birth is essential for a complete understanding of the normal pattern of development and for a realisation in what can happen on distorting this pattern.

Today there is extensive evidence to show how conditions in the prenatal environment can and do affect development before birth. This has justified beginning the study of development from the moment of conception rather than from the time of birth.

Most of the development that takes place before birth has been investigated by physiologists and members of the medical profession. Their contributions have for the most part been to supplement the physiological and physical data with evidence of the effects of psychological states on the pattern of development and the long-term effects of the attitudes of significant people.

Therefore, it is essential that the couples who desire to begin a family be better guided and that they be in a favourable state of mind and body before and after that significant moment of conception. Their attitudes and other significant people's attitudes will have a long-term influence on the child.

It is better that the parents and others understand the significance and the important characteristics of the prenatal period.

The hereditary endowment, which serves as the foundation for later development is fixed once and at the time of conception. According to Douglas and Holland, "One's heredity consists of all the structures, physical characteristics, functions or capacities derived from parents, other ancestry or species."

The sex of the child is fixed at the time of conception. Sex depends on the kind of spermatozoon that unites with the ovum. The conditions within the mother's body will not affect it as is true of the hereditary endowment.

The above characteristics make two points very clear. (1) The inherited characteristics are always transmitted through the respective genes at the time of conception. (2) The sex of the child is fixed at the time of conception and it will not change. The mother has no influence on the sex of the child. The sex depends on the kind of spermatozoon that unites with the ovum.

Proportionally greater growth and development take place during the prenatal period than at any other time throughout the individual's entire life. During the nine months before birth, the individual grows from a microscopically small cell to an infant who measures approximately twenty inches in length and weighs on the average 7 pounds. It has been estimated that weight during this time increases eleven million times. Development is likewise phenomenally rapid.

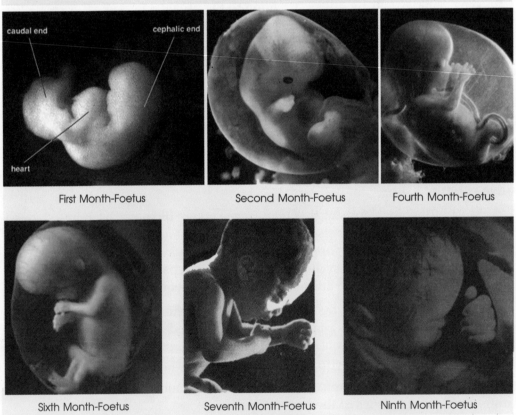

MIRACLE OF LIFE

caudal end   cephalic end

heart

First Month-Foetus   Second Month-Foetus   Fourth Month-Foetus

Sixth Month-Foetus   Seventh Month-Foetus   Ninth Month-Foetus

Fig. 2.2. Development of foetus from first month to the ninth month in the mother's womb

Favourable conditions in the mother's body can foster the development of hereditary potentials while unfavourable conditions can stunt their development even to the point of distorting the pattern of future development. At few if met any other times in the lifespan are hereditary potentials so influenced by environmental conditions as they are during the prenatal period.

The prenatal period is the time when significant people form attitudes toward newly created individuals. These attitudes will have a marked influence on the way these individuals are treated especially during their early formative years. If the attitudes are heavily emotionally weighted, they can often play havoc with the mother's homeostasis and by doing so upset the conditions in the mother's body that are essential to the normal development of the newly created individual.

Thus it is important that the mother has a favourable environment while she is carrying the foetus. If so, the newly created individual develops in a favourable condition both physically and psychologically.

"The environment is everything that affects the individual except his genes." Say, Boring, Langfield and Weld.

The environment consists of the external forces which influence the growth and development of an individual right from his conception. Before birth, the mother's womb is the place where these forces play their part. The nutrition is received by the embryo through the blood stream of the mother. So the mother needs to have a well balanced diet rich in proteins and other vitamins and minerals. This is where one can pause and see how many mothers follow this, and how many mothers are privileged to have a balanced diet and how many mothers go hungry. In some cultures, if the child is not wanted, the mothers are purposely not fed so that the

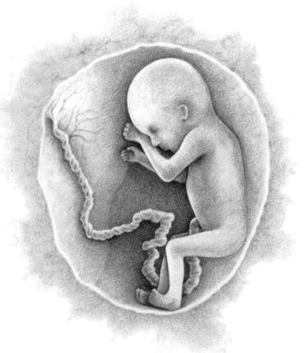

Fig. 2.3. Foetus attached with umbilical cord to the placenta in the mother's womb

pregnancy will be terminated. Many children are born with many physical problems due to the lack of balanced diet of the mother. In some cultures mothers are fed well by the in-laws if the baby is going to be a boy while the mothers are starved almost to death if the baby is going to be a girl.

This is one area where the parents as well as the in-laws and other significant people need guidance and counselling. EVERY LIFE IS PRECIOUS. Whether it is a boy or a girl no one has the right to destroy a life. Thousands of foetuses are killed through abortions and by other means. This is wrong. The parents and other significant people like the in-laws are responsible for such crimes. In some countries abortion is made legal while in other countries abortion is illegal. But let me make it clear that it is not the country and its legal system which is responsible for the life

Fig. 2.4. Girl Child – The beautiful creation of God !

of an innocent and helpless being. The responsibility for the life of a helpless being solely lies on the parents. These days many young couples go through the tragedy of guilt due to their own selfishness. It is God who gives life and let us take care of this life with respect and love for each human being.

Sometimes it is very encouraging to see some proud fathers who are eagerly waiting for the arrival of a daughter while others are so proud of their daughters. For instance, when Indira Gandhi was born her grandfather Motilal Nehru remarked that she will be worth a 100 sons.

Dear Parents, let us not forget that the girl child has a equal right to life just like the boys.

SOME COMMON PHYSICAL HAZARDS DURING PRENATAL PERIOD

According to Havighurst, "What happens to the foetus in the womb and in the process of its birth, the adequacy of its uterine nutrition, its good or ill fortune at birth with regard to infection or injury, all these often prove as important as its heredity."

MATERNAL MALNUTRITION

Serious malformation of eyes, ears, heart and brain can occur due to maternal malnutrition, vitamin and glandular deficiencies. Excessive use of drugs, radiation, smoking and drinking, infectious diseases, diabetes, German measles etc. can cause serious malformation of eyes, ears, heart and brain.

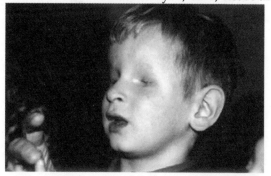

Fig. 2.5. Maternal malnutrition can cause physical hazards such as visual and audio impairment in children

Fig. 2.6. Physical malformation caused due to maternal malnutrition in children

Malnutrition and dehydration during pregnancy may damage the developing foetal brain causing learning difficulties, especially reading disabilities. It is also seen that such children are restless and they find it difficult to concentrate and comprehend. Damage to the foetal brain due to whatever cause, will have effects on the individual's behaviour that become more and more apparent as children grow older and are compared with other children of the same age.

Fig. 2.7. Disabilities of reading

MATERNAL AGE

From mid 30's on, there will be a danger to pregnancy especially if the women had no earlier pregnancies. As women approach the menopause, they frequently have endocrine disorders which slow down the development of the embryo and foetus causing cretinism, Down's syndrome, heart malformations and hydro-cephalus all of which involve physical and mental defects. Older women also tend to have smaller babies and have more complications at birth than do younger women. Paternal age may cause developmental irregularities or still-births only when paternal age is over sixty years.

Certain female hormones, such as oestrogens and progesterones, when taken in the early stages of pregnancy may disturb the normal cardiovascular development of the foetus and cause congenital heart diseases.

Chemicals and other hazards faced by women working in places like hospitals, beauty parlours and factories may be responsible for the increasing number of birth defects and

Fig. 2.8. Down Syndrome due to maternal age

miscarriages. Miscarriages are always possible up to the fifth month of pregnancy. The most vulnerable time is when the woman's menstrual period would normally occur.

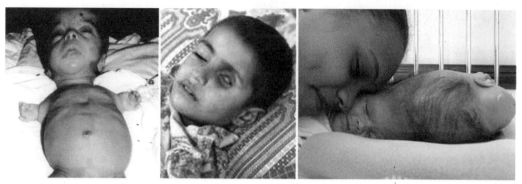

Fig. 2.9. Various birth defects due to chemicals and other hazards

The other causes for miscarriages are, falls, accidents, emotional shocks, malnutrition, glandular disturbances, vitamin deficiency and serious diseases like pneumonia and diabetes. Miscarriages that are due to unfavourable conditions in the prenatal environment are likely to occur, between the tenth and eleventh weeks after conception.

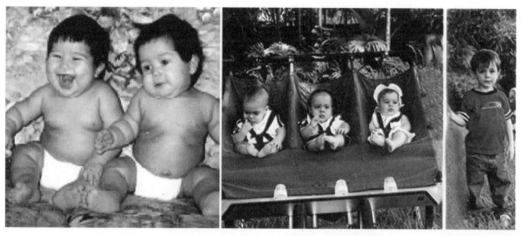

Fig. 2.10. Twins   Fig. 2.11. Triplets   Fig. 2.12. Single

Multiple births are more hazardous than single births. Complications during delivery especially maternal stress affects uterine contractions and is likely to lead to complications during birth.

If developmental irregularities are serious and if the embryo or foetus does not miscarry or die at birth or shortly afterwards, the individual will be deformed in some way. Some deformities are not diagnosed until months or even years after birth. Epilepsy, cerebral palsy and mental deficiency may not show up until babyhood or even early childhood.

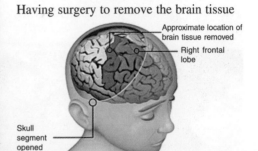

A VICTIM OF EPILEPSY

Having surgery to remove the brain tissue

Approximate location of brain tissue removed

Right frontal lobe

Skull segment opened

Fig. 2.13. Children affected by Cerebral Palsy   Fig. 2.14. Epilepsy can be treated by surgery

Parents find it difficult to accept a defective child and blame themselves for having caused the defect. This will result in strong feelings of guilt and a tendency either to overprotect or refuse to accept the defective child.

This is the other area where the parents need guidance and counselling to accept the defective children and to help these children make proper adjustments educationally, psychologically and vocationally.

Not only the physiological state of the mother but also the psychological state of the mother during pregnancy, her habits and interests are all important for the well being of the baby within the womb.

The favourable (positive) attitudes of the parents, grandparents, other siblings and other significant people have a positive effect on the baby before birth and this tends to be persistent after the baby's birth.

THE EFFECTS OF ATTITUDES OF SIGNIFICANT PEOPLE ON CHILDREN — BEFORE AND AFTER BIRTH

Fig. 2.15. Happy couple delighted at the expected arrival of the baby

The mother's attitude can have an effect on her unborn baby not through the umbilical cord, which is the only direct connection between the two but as a result of endocrine changes which can and do occur if the mother is subjected to severe and prolonged stress which normally accompanies, persistently unfavourable attitudes. Favourable attitudes, by contrast will lead to good body homeostasis and this will favour normal development during the prenatal period.

Fig. 2.16. Happy and loving family environment for holistic growth of children

After birth the mother's attitudes, most of which were formed before the baby's birth, have an influence because they are reflected in the way the child is treated.

Nancy, a school teacher (name changed) complained of her seven-year-old daughter's daily bedwetting problem. During her sharing, she stressed that her daughter was given everything she wanted. I asked Nancy, whether she genuinely accepted her daughter. To this also she responded positively. So, I told her may be unconsciously she was not accepting her daughter or she might be having some negative attitude towards her which she was not aware of. Perhaps, she could reflect about it sometime. Nancy went home after the school was over and the next morning, before the morning assembly, she met me to share the happy news that her daughter didn't wet the bed and she had a sound sleep last night. She was in a good mood of sharing everything openly. From her sharing it was revealed that she was forced by her in-laws, (her father-in-law was a senior medical practitioner)to abort the foetus. They didn't want her to have a baby at that time. She tried to abort the child, but didn't succeed and she gave birth to a baby girl. To be true, Nancy herself accepted her daughter only that night and that was the first time her seven-year-old daughter felt that she was wanted and accepted by her parents. The emotional security which she felt made her to sleep well without wetting the bed.

SOME NEGATIVE ATTITUDES WHICH WILL LEAD TO PSYCHOLOGICAL HAZARDS DURING PRENATAL PERIOD

MATERNAL STRESS :

Maternal stress over a period of time can cause psychological hazards. This stress may be due to fear, anxiety, anger, grief, jealousy and shock. Maternal stress affects the developing child before and after birth. Before birth, severe and persistent glandular imbalance due to stress may result in irregularities in the developing child and complications of delivery or even prematurity. Maternal anxiety affects uterine contractions with the result that labour lasts longer than normal and the chances of complications are greater because the infant must often be delivered by instruments. Further more, anxiety often leads to over eating and excessive weight gain in pregnancy which further complicates birth.

Some studies have shown that when prolonged emotional strain affects endocrine balance, anxieties may carry over into the period of the newborn and seriously affect adjustments to postnatal life. The infant may show hyperactivity which prevents its adjusting to feeding and sleeping patterns or it may cry excessively. Prolonged and extreme maternal stress during the period of the foetus frequently causes more illness during the first three years of the child's life than is experienced by children who had a more favourable foetal environment. Children whose mothers were under great stress during pregnancy may show more anxiety and this has an adverse effect on their ability to learn, to remember and to reason to their full capacities. As a result they may be less bright as compared to other children.

Another serious effect of maternal stress during pregnancy is on children's post-natal adjustment to family members, because they are considered as difficult babies due to their hyperactivity and excessive crying and moodiness. The attitudes of family members towards them are then less favourable. As they grow older these children sense these unfavourable attitudes not only on the family members but on the part of peers, teachers and other outsiders. Feeling unloved and rejected they often show below average physical development, hyperactivity, lag in developing motor skills and speech and learning problems. This may result in poor personal and social adjustments.

The other points on the part of both the parents and other significant people may be not wanting the child because the child is illegitimate or not wanting the child at that particular time due to parents own educational or professional plans.

Preference for a male child by parents and grandparents will make the unborn child, if a girl, as already rejected, unwanted and unloved.

The siblings too generally wish a child of their own sex whom they regard as more likely to be a playmate. Many parents and grandparents may wish that their baby be perfect in every way; mentally, physically, emotionally and be obedient, beautiful and bright. These wishes can colour their attitudes towards the unborn baby. Not wanting a multiple birth or wishing to have a miscarriage or an abortion have very serious adverse effect on the child before and after the birth.

Most of these points are already discussed earlier. To make it clear again the parents need guidance and counselling to accept their unborn infants with love and care. After they are born many parents need guidance to accept and care for their children. It is very sad to see in many cases the children are told that they were not wanted and the mother had attempted abortion.

To cite another example, once I had some contact with an eighteen-year-old girl for a year. She was very pretty to look at. She was talented in music and dance and good at studies too. But she had a floating sadness on her face. When I had a meeting with her parents they revealed the horrifying news that the mother had attempted abortion three times to abort her and they had already shared this with their daughter. In my heart I questioned quite violently and asked myself, "How could they do such a crime to a very lovely being." The next one year both the parents and the daughter went through the counselling sessions and today all three of them and her brother are happily living together and she is one of the top entrepreneurs of our country.

SOME FAVOURABLE CONDITIONS WHICH WOULD HELP THE COUPLES TO START A FAMILY

- **sound physical and mental health.**

- **genuine desire to have children.**

- **love for children.**

- **sound economic and emotional stability.**

- **share the responsibility to look after the children.**

WORKING MOTHERS :

— See that one of the grandparents is available to look after your child during the daytime during the first two years.

— Please ensure that you are with your child at night during the critical age of infancy.

Infancy can be and is one of the happiest periods of life. It is not the quantity of time but the quality that matters, which a mother spends with her child. Studies

Fig. 2.17. Working mother

Fig. 2.18. Childcare should be shared both by mother and father

have shown that mothers who were educated and employed spent more time with their children at the expense of their spare time and sleep. They are happy to cuddle and love them and even tolerate their crying.

Babyhood is regarded as the critical period in personality development because it is the time when the foundations of adult personality are laid. Therefore the presence of parents with their infants has a great influence on their continuous development.

CHAPTER 3

INFANCY

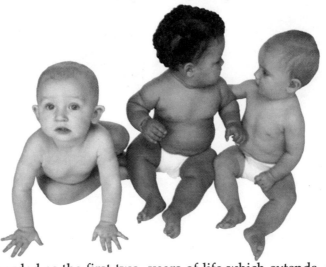

I nfancy is regarded as the first two years of life which extends from the end of the second week to the end of the second year of life. Infancy is known as the True Foundation Age because it is at this time many behaviour patterns, many attitudes and many patterns of emotional expressions are being established.

Freud maintained that personality maladjustments in adulthood had their origins in unfavourable childhood experiences. Erikson also contented that "Childhood is the scene of man's beginning as man, the place where our particular virtues and vices slowly but clearly develop and make themselves felt". He added how infants are treated will determine whether they will develop "basic trust" or "basic distrust" - viewing the world as safe, reliable, and nurturing or as full of threat, unpredictability, and treachery.

Fig. 3.1. A healthy child

Fig. 3.2. Healthy environment is necessary for growth of a healthy child

The first two years are critical in setting the pattern for personal and social adjustments. Providing a rich social life for a $1\frac{1}{2}$ years old child is the best thing you can do to guarantee a good mind.

Certain characteristics of infancy while similar to characteristics of other periods in the lifespan, are of particular importance during the infancy years.

PHYSICAL DEVELOPMENT

Infancy is the period of rapid growth, change and development. Inner as well as outer organs develop rapidly and there is fast growth in terms of height, weight and size. There is intensive motor activity and restlessness. Muscle control follows the laws of developmental direction. The earliest skills to be learned are the head, arm and hand skills. Due to their inability to speak during the major part of infancy, babies communications are mainly in pre-speech forms - crying, babbling, gestures and emotional expressions.

Fig. 3.3. Muscular movement is necessary for child's growth

DEPENDENCE AND SELF-ASSERTION

Although the child is a helpless one and depends upon others for the satisfaction of his basic needs, he is quite self-assertive.

Fig. 3.4. Dependency   Fig. 3.5. Self assertion

Even for his emotional satisfaction, he depends upon others. He expects that everybody around him should love him and give him his entire affection and attention. He wants to love and to be loved and in this exchange he totally depends on the mercy of others. At the same time he is quite self-assertive. He tries to dominate his superiors and elders. His wishes must be fulfilled. He thinks he is always right and everyone around him should obey him. He tries to assert himself all the time in all situations. In this way the child at this stage is dependent but as he moves into the later years he slowly gains individuality and independence.

MENTAL DEVELOPMENT

The child at this stage is very curious and is an explorer. During the infancy stage, the child is very curious about knowing everything around him and he wants to explore everything and pull out all that is at his reach. He is in the habit of asking questions like what is this? Why does it happen ? etc. Answers do not interest him as much as asking questions. His speed of questioning is so rapid that he doesn't wait for the previous questions' answers.

Fig. 3.6. Mental curiosity in children

The child at this stage is very immature in intelligence. He can't reason and can't do abstract thinking. He can only think in concrete terms. His power of observation, perception and concentration are also not developed. Yet he has a very good memory. He can cram and reproduce the matter easily.

It is also a period of make-believe and fantasy. They live in the world of their own creation. This is a period of rich but baseless imagination. The infant has limited potentialities and aspires more than what he can actually get in actual life. He compensates himself in fantasy and make-believe.

Infancy is characterized by creativity. He develops a creative attitude and often engages himself in making or collecting so many things.

The time concept and the concept of distance are not developed. For him, today, yesterday and a month after are the same as tomorrow. So also, the places like Delhi and London are on the next door for him. Understanding comes from a combination of sensory exploration and motor manipulation.

EMOTIONAL DEVELOPMENT

Infancy is the period of emotional instability. This period is characterized by

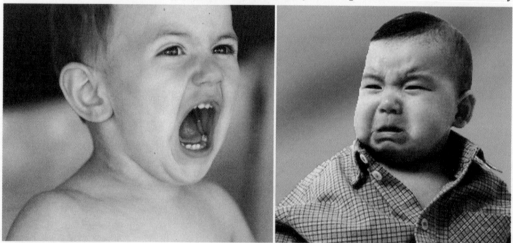

Fig. 3.7. Emotions in babyhood

violent emotional experiences with intensity and frequency. They are spontaneous and the infant is hardly able to exercise control over them. He is not able to hide his feelings and in this way the emotional expressions are in overt form. Temper tantrums are quite often if his wishes are not fulfilled.

SOCIAL DEVELOPMENT

Early social foundations are important, first, because the type of behaviour the infants show in social situations affects their personal and

Fig. 3.8. Children learn social behaviour

social adjustments and second, because once established, these patterns tend to persist. In infancy the child is almost completely ego-centric, selfish and unsocial. He doesn't want to share his toys or give any of his possessions to anyone else. He wants to have all the things, even love, admiration and affection reserved for him. He does not care for the social and moral codes and principles and places his self-interest at the premium.

SEXUAL DEVELOPMENT

Although the sex organs at this stage are not fully developed yet the sex tendency is in a continuous stage of development. The findings of psychoanalysts like Freud and others have clearly shown that the sexual life of the infant is as rich as that of an adolescent. An infant passes through the three stages of sexual development - stage of self-love, homosexual and heterosexual. At the initial stage, the child derives pleasure from his/her own body by sucking his/her thumb or touching the sex organs. Later on he/she seeks the satisfaction of his/her sex impulse outside and develops sentiments of love for the mother or father depending upon his/her sex. Finally the child develops heterosexual tendency and in this respect the male child gets himself attached to the mother and the female child to the father.

GUIDANCE FOR PARENTS AND OTHERS WHO HANDLE THE INFANTS

From the guidance point of view, it is better for the parents and others to become aware of some of the common hazards the infants face and how these hazards can be handled properly.

Fig. 3.9. Eating habits

EATING HABITS

Infants who suck for longer periods show signs of tenseness. They engage in more non-nutritive sucking such as thumb sucking, have more difficulties in sleep and are more restless than those whose sucking periods are shorter. If weaning is delayed, infants are likely to resist new kinds of food and substitute thumb sucking for the nipple.

Fig. 3.10. Sleep habits

SLEEPING HABITS

Crying, strenuous play with an adult or noise and sounds from firecrackers etc. can make babies tense and keep them from falling asleep.

THE HABITS OF ELIMINATION

These habits cannot be established until the nerves and muscles have developed adequately. Trying to toilet train babies too early will make them uncooperative about establishing these habits when they are maturationally ready. Delay in toilet training, on the other hand, results in habits of irregularity and lack of motivation on the baby's part. Enuresis - bed-wetting is common when training is not timed according to the baby's developmental readiness.

Most of the serious psychological hazards of babyhood are related either directly or indirectly to the failure to master the developmental tasks of babyhood.

Delayed speech, like delayed motor control is serious in infancy because at this age the foundations are being laid for the development of the tools of communication that will be needed later as social horizons broaden. Due to delayed speech the child may find himself out of place in the company of other children or an outsider .

Fig. 3.11. Speech development in children

There are a number of reasons for delayed speech, the most common of which are low level of intelligence, lack of stimulation and multiple births. When parents and others fail to stimulate the early attempts to speak, most infants lose interest in trying to speak. The result is that their speech is often marked delayed. On the contrary, when babies are encouraged to babble and to learn to say words, their speech development conforms to the normal pattern and is often accelerated. The more the novelty there is in the environment, the greater is the baby's motivation to vocalize. In some cases, a child who was very talkative may reduce talking to a great extent when a new sibling arrives at home.

Therefore parents and other family members can stimulate and motivate in the speech development of children. Children are great imitators. In today's home environment, the various T.V. channels are a great stimulator for the infant's speech development and they do imitate the language, expressions etc. At the same time certain programmes are harmful for them. Parents do need to censor the various programmes which children watch.

THE IMPACT OF TELEVISION (TV) ON CHILDREN

The present day media especially TV with all its glamorous, news saturated glossy presentation is ensnaring and encroaching the minds, sense and sensibility of the human life.

While this is true for all the age groups, it is having a larger than life effect over the school going child.

While a TV at home opens a world of information and education to the young mind, uncensored and unguided viewing by the innocent

Fig. 3.12. Children watching television

mind can lead to serious mishaps that will have a devastating and sometimes lasting effect on the child's personality. For example, the little child is engrossed in cartoons like - Pokemon, Scooby-Doo, while these programs produce lots of entertainment and joy, the child slowly shifts from the world of reality to the world of fantasy. His entire life seems to revolve around such cartoon characters.

Today we have 'Pokemon' branded school bags, tiffin boxes, books, notebooks, pencil boxes, water bottles and other items. The child is preoccupied with playing games like "Dragonballs" which are the direct outputs of such cartoons rather than doing useful work like reading or pursuing habits like painting or drawing.

A few years back due to telecast of a series of serials and movies involving imaginary characters like Superman and Batman, there were tragic incidents where little children had been injured or even had succumbed to death while trying to 'fly' like their imaginary heroes.

The recent hanging of Dhananjoy Chatterjee was widely covered in the electronic and print media. This coverage evoked the public interest throughout the country. In West Bengal, children started to enact the entire sequence of hanging and in the process of playing out the drama, a child in the role of Dhananjoy got strangled, while his other playmates helplessly watched on.

Fig. 3.13. Children imitating their super heroes

The children's play interests have also shifted from harmless games to the more injurious ones. The little ones imitate their screen heroes, speaking in or so called 'macho dialect' and playing games, walking and interacting with guns, pistols and blood thirsty weapons.

Perhaps the effect of TV is most frightening on the little minds when we hear them talk. Even a small Kindergarten child now unhesitatingly talks about taboo subjects like 'sex' or uses abusive vulgar language.

It is indeed a subject of great consternation that we are not realizing that we are gifting our children an everlasting ugly future full of unpredictable and disastrous prospects.

Few healthy measures to check children from watching unhealthy programmes would be, parents censuring the programmes and having child-lock facility in some TVs. This facility prevents direct access to certain channels by children. These selected channels can only be accessed by executing special procedures known only to parents.

The positive effects of TV are also worth mentioning. The level of knowledge is enhanced in various areas through some recommended channels like Discovery, Animal Planet, Pogo, National Geographic, BBC and History. Better scientific concepts are learned through visuals and explanations. For example, Space Studies, Oceanic Flora and Fauna, Expeditions to Antarctica and Arctic.

EMOTIONAL INSECURITY IN CHILDREN

Children who are deprived of normal emotions especially affection, acceptance, curiosity and joy do not thrive physically. If emotional deprivation is severe and

Fig. 3.14. Children in emotional insecurity

prolonged, it inhibits the secretion of the pituitary hormones including the growth hormones and this may lead to what has been called "deprivation dwarfism". They usually become listless, depressed and apathetic and often develop nervous mannerisms such as thumb sucking.

Prolonged unpleasant emotional states such as fear or anger can cause endocrine changes which upset body homeostasis. This, then, is reflected in eating and sleeping difficulties, in nervous mannerisms such as excessive thumb sucking and in excessive crying. There are many causes of stress: poor health, parental neglect, and poor environmental conditions that interfere with proper sleeping and eating habits. Constant and close association with a nervous and tense mother is a particularly important factor.

On the other hand too much affection from parents can encourage their infants to focus their attention on themselves and to become self bound and selfish. Infants thus expect others to show affection for them but they do not reciprocate. In infants, timidity may persist long after babyhood if a shy or fearful child is exposed to too many strangers or too many frightening situations.

Children who are separated from their mothers develop feelings of insecurity which are expressed in personality disturbances that may lay the foundation for later maladjustments.

Fig. 3.15. A family in conflict

The deterioration in family relationships that always occurs during the second year of life is psychologically hazardous because infants notice that family members have changed attitudes toward them and treat them differently. As a result, they usually have unloved and rejected feelings which lead to resentment and insecurity.

Overprotectiveness can lead to school phobia and excessive shyness in the presence of strangers.

When parents are unhappy and when there is a frictional relationship existing between them, some babies become the target of anger and resentment. The infants are either neglected or abused. Thus a healthy relationship between parents help in the healthy development of children.

There are various causes for unhappiness in infants like poor health, teething, need for independence and attention. When parents start disciplining the children, child abuse, sibling rivalry and resentment are seen.

Infants who are in poor health, either temporarily or chronically, do not feel up to the mark and as a result tend to be fretful and irritable. Periodic discomfort due to teething causes babies to be fretful and negativistic. When parental discipline is harsh, babies feel unloved and unwanted. Increased sibling resentment is seen when the elder sister or brother has to care for the younger one. This causes unhappiness in babies. In large families where the care of babies is often in the hands of an older female sibling, babies have reason to experience frequent periods of unhappiness because they are aware of how their sister feels about them and how they resent having to play the role of a surrogate parent.

The first year of life can be and is one of the happiest for an individual's life. The dependency of young babies make them appealing to children as well as to adults. Most children like to play with them while adults not only want to cuddle and love them but are happy to tolerate their crying and the other disruptions their care brings into their lives. By contrast, for almost all the infants the second year of life is far less happier than the first.

Infancy is regarded as a critical period in personality development because it is the time when the foundations of adult personality are laid. Therefore, the importance of parent-child relationship has a great role during this period.

CHAPTER 4

HABIT FORMATION IN CHILDREN

WHAT IS HABIT FORMATION ?

Habit is something that a person does often. Habits are actions of a person which become very easy and mechanical for him. It becomes automatic for him. Habits are the product of experiences and practice. In the beginning it may require a voluntary and deliberate effort on the part of the individual. One's way of walking, talking, certain body movements etc., are such habits.

Various experts have given definitions of habit. Few of them are given below:

"A habitual action is the result of many repetitions of the act in approximately the same way. It is done without conscious thought, performed smoothly and with the maximum speed required."

— Ryburn

"Habit is the name given to behaviour so often repeated as to be automatic."

— Garret

SOME CHARACTERISTICS OF HABITS :

1. Habits are acquired. They are not innate or inherited.

2. Habits are learned through continuous practice.

3. Habits are uniform actions. They are performed everytime almost the same way.

4. Habits are very prompt and automatic.

5. Habits are performed very easily and mechanically.

6. There is recurrency in habits.

7. Habits can be performed with least attention even while talking. For example, women do knitting while talking. These days some attend to the mobile calls as they do their work.

8. Habits reduce fatigue. For example, a driver who is used to distant driving, doesn't become too tired of driving.

9. Those who are used to habitual actions possess a strong tendency against change or modification.

10. Habits are not confined only to conative acts but also have a wide operation to one's thoughts and feelings too.

11. Habits are useful as well as harmful. Habits are divided into good habits and bad habits. Good habits are like being truthful, punctual, honest etc. There are bad habits like drinking, smoking, lying, truancy etc.

12. Nervous system is the base of habits. The nervous system is the principal factor in formation of habits. "Nerves carry messages", to and from the brain. When approximately the same message is taken to the brain, and the same answer comes back, for the same action to result, a kind of tract is worn, so that the answer to the message carried to the brain becomes more and more automatic. It becomes more difficult for any other answer to come to the in-going message than the one that has been given again and again in response to what is approximately the same message. Thus the basis of habit is this groove, as it were, which is born in the nerves."

— Ryburn

HOW WE CAN FORM GOOD HABITS IN CHILDREN ?

A school going child is made to wake up at 5:30 a.m. daily by the parents. In due course of time, when the child completes the 1st term of his class I, he wakes up by himself without any effort. It has already become a habit for him to wake up at 5:30 a.m. whether there is school or not.

THE QUESTION IS WHO ARE RESPONSIBLE FOR GOOD HABIT FORMATION IN CHILDREN ?

The main persons responsible for good habit formation in children are :

Parents, grandparents and other elders in the family. Then the teachers and all those who are associated with children in the school.

What else ? The good examples of parents and elders and from the teachers are sources of good habits. Children learn through imitation. So whatever the parents, the other siblings and elders do, the children imitate. For example, if parents are regular in getting up early in the morning and retire on time to bed, children also follow the same habit without any hesitation.

The examples of teachers are great sources for good habit formation. Children though very young are very observant to see, which teacher is very punctual and hardworking etc.

Besides parents' and teachers' examples, there are other factors too which help in the formation of good habits in children.

A good curriculum with lots of stimulating activities help children to learn good habits like using the time well, hardworking, team spirit, co-operation, punctuality etc.

Many family and social activities at home also help children to learn good habits. For example, family gatherings on grandparents birthday, parents birthday and

Fig. 4.1. Lending a helping hand

other siblings birthday etc., help children develop good habits like respect for others appreciation, sharing, caring and generosity.

The following practical points will be useful in the formation of good habits in children :

1. Begin habit formation in early age

The younger the child the greater the receptivity of the mind. As said earlier, the child is a good imitator. For him, parents, elders and teachers are everything. Once the child is in school, whatever the teacher tells is more important than parents at home. So the inculcation of right habits in children should be started as early as possible so that they may be saved from picking up wrong habits, behaviour, thoughts and feelings early in life as well as later in life.

Fig. 4.2. Child greeting an elder

2. Encourage the children to have a firm determination and initiative

'Where there is a will there is a way'. If a child of class II wishes or decides to wake up at 5:15 a.m. instead of 5:30 a.m. and revise his lessons, encourage him to launch his new habit of waking up at 5:15 a.m. A public announcement by the child that he would get up early at 5:15 a.m. to revise his lessons or to do a little extra reading can be a powerful initiative to start with and is a less burden for the parents. It provides a strong emotional stimulus and ego involvement for the child. Give a word of praise to him for his strong determination.

3. Encourage positive attitude in children

Every initiative by the child for a good cause should be praised and encouraged whether he succeeded in his initiative or not. This helps in developing a positive attitude towards life and honest effort even if he fails in his attempt. It will result in his sincere effort again and succeed. Every good behaviour and conduct should be appreciated.

4. Give reasonable appreciation at the right time

A child should be praised for his good work but not over praised, or don't indulge in giving such expensive gifts. Praise the child without any delay, at the right time. Don't wait for a week or a month to show him that you appreciate him.

5. Encourage the child to set up definite specification for the new habit

It is of no use in saying that from tomorrow onwards I'll work hard for all the subjects. This is too general and too vague a decision. Instead, if the child decides that from tomorrow onwards he is going to study the subject Hindi first, which he doesn't like, and starts studying it, he is specific and sincere about his new habit.

6. Use the first opportunity to act

If the day fixed tommorrow, is a Saturday to start studying Hindi first, then on

Saturday, the first thing the child has to do is to learn Hindi first before studying any other subject. Otherwise he'll lose interest again in this subject. So don't wait for another tomorrow.

7. Parents and other elders see that the child is on the right track

When a child starts an attempt to form a new habit, the parents need to watch him and direct him carefully so that he doesn't follow a wrong track. Children are so innocent and immature while starting something new. Therefore, guiding him to follow the right direction is a must.

8. Follow consistency in encouragement and corrective measures

All those who are involved in a child's life should be consistent or follow the same measure of encouragement and at the right time when a child does something right. In the same way if a child does something wrong, put it as wrong or as an undesirable behaviour by all. Sometimes, it can happen that some lenient parents may approve or don't even correct the child when he has done something wrong. While in the school, the child may be corrected for the same undesirable behaviour. This will cause such confusion in the child and the child may start disliking the teacher and the school in such a situation. Sometimes, the grandparents may become so overprotective of their grandchild and he may not be corrected at all. A child may be appreciated by the teacher for the improvement he has made in his behaviour but the parents may be demanding, and may neglect to praise the child for the same improvement he has made. This kind of inconsistency of behaviour from any part, either from the school or from home may affect the proper development of good habit in children. Therefore, consistency in encouraging a child or correcting a child is a necessary standard of action for good habit formation in children.

9. Sufficient practice and repetition

'Practice makes a person perfect.' So, for the habit fomation, it is essential that action should be repeated frequently in the same manner under similar circumstances. They must be made to make persistent efforts in practising a particular mode of behaviour (action, thought or feeling) until it is established into a habit. For example, listen silently while others are speaking.

10. Use preventive measure for formation of good habits

It is always said, 'be on time,' or be five minutes earlier for any task you have to do. If children are taught to be in school at least five minutes before the first bell for morning assembly see that the child is in the school before the 1st bell or if a student has to submit a particular assignment in school on Monday morning, see that the assignment is ready by Saturday night or at least by Sunday morning. It helps in time management as well as in having a pleasant satisfaction in the student. This will also ensure a child to have some relaxing and refreshing activities before he starts the next week of school.

If the above measures of good habit formation are followed, there will not be any need for behaviour modification of a child by a psychologist or a psychiatrist.

In conclusion, we can say that both the parents and teachers need to work together for good habit formation in children. It is the duty of the parents, elders and teachers to provide a good and rich environment to children from the time they are very young. Their own life should be a model for inculcation of good habits among children. Parents, other elders and teachers are the role models for youngsters.

CHAPTER 5

Early Childhood

Fig. 5.1. Children in early childhood

INTRODUCTION

Childhood is widely sub-divided into two periods — early childhood and late childhood.

Early childhood extends from two to six years. Thus early childhood begins at the conclusion of babyhood - the age when dependency is practically a thing of the past and is being replaced by growing independence and ends about the time the child enters first grade in school.

This dividing line between early and late childhood is significant because in our culture the law requires that children must begin their formal education when they reach their sixth birthday. Social pressures and social expectations play an important role in determining how children differ before they enter school from those who have already been subjected to school experiences. If formal entrance into school came a year earlier or a year later, the dividing line between early and late childhood would be at five years in the formal case, and at seven in the later case.

The new pressures and expectations that accompany the child's formal entrance into school result in changes in patterns of behaviour, interests and values. As a result, children become "different" from what they were earlier. It is this difference in their psychological make up rather than the difference in their physical make up that justifies dividing this long span of years into two sub-divisions, early and later childhood.

Fig. 5.2. Early childhood activities

The major aspects of growth and development at this stage are - physical, mental, emotional, social, cultural, sexual, religious and moral development.

PHYSICAL DEVELOPMENT

Early childhood is characterized as the period of slow, steady and uniform

Fig. 5.3. Physical activities of early childhood

growth as compared with the rapid rate of growth in infancy. Though, it is a time of relatively even growth, there are seasonal variations for example, July to mid-December is the most favourable time for increase in weight and April to mid-August is most favourable for height. Development rate although, continuous and uniform, is very slow at this stage.

Body proportions change markedly and the "baby look" disappears. Facial features remain small but the chin becomes more pronounced and the neck elongates.

Differences in body build become apparent for the first time in early childhood. Some children have an endomorphic or flabby, fat body build, some have a mesomorphic or sturdy muscular body build and some have an ectomorphic or relatively thin body build. The bones ossify at different rates in different parts of the body, following the laws of developmental direction. The muscles become larger, stronger and heavier, with the result that children look thinner as early childhood

Fig. 5.4. Children on monkey bars

progresses, even though they weigh more. During the first four to six months of early childhood, the last four baby teeth - the back molars erupt. During the last half year of early childhood, baby teeth begin to be replaced by permanent teeth.

SPEECH DEVELOPMENT

By the time children are two years old, most of the pre-speech forms of communication they found so useful during infancy have been abandoned. Young children no longer babble and their crying is greatly curtailed. They may use gestures but mainly as supplements to speech to emphasize the meaning of the words they use. There is a strong motivation on the part of most children to learn to speak. Learning to speak is an essential tool in socialization. During this period, rapid strides are made in building up vocabulary, mastering pronunciation and combining words into sentences. Certain sounds and sound combinations are especially difficult for a young child to learn to pronounce such as the consonants, z,w,d, s and g and the consonant combinations st, str, dr, and fl. Yet, exceptions are seen in small children due to their exposure to TV and other childhood activities. Their vocabulary increases rapidly as they learn new words and new meanings. Three to five - word sentences are used as early as two years of age. Early childhood is popularly known as the chatterbox age.

INTELLECTUAL DEVELOPMENT

This stage is the period of intellectual advancement. The rate of intellectual development is quite rapid at this stage which resembles the rate of physical growth at infancy. The child learns much during this period. Vocabulary develops and the child continues to talk incessantly. The how and why questions are more predominant now. Memory and imagination continues to be strong and active.

Fig. 5.5. Intellectually stimulating activities   Fig. 5.6. Intense observation

But there is inability to distinguish between products of memory and imagination. The concept of time still means little to the child. Children use the present before they use the future and the past. Abstract thinking is not developed, and the child learns by trial and error, by imitation and by seeing the concrete objects. He learns by repetition, drill and by rote memory.

INTERESTS

This is what a five-year-old boy said, "I want to be a traffic police man when I grow up", (both the parents are doctors).

The child's vocational choice is based on what is important for the child at that time. Early interest in their future vocations is centred on jobs children regard as glamorous, exciting and prestigious or which embody activities or uniforms that are important to them at that time. But their interest will change by the time they reach early adolescence.

I have decided to be a navy officer.   Why do you want to be a navy officer?   because I like the uniform.

I want to be a fighter plane pilot.   What made you to take that decision?   I want to kill our enemies.

Fig. 5.7. Interests of children in early childhood

EMOTIONAL DEVELOPMENT

The common emotions are anger, fear, jealousy, curiosity, envy, joy and grief. Emotions are especially intense during early childhood. This is a time of disequilibrium when children are "out of focus" in the sense that they are easily aroused to emotional outbursts and as a result are difficult to live with and guide. While this is true for the major part of early childhood, it is especially true of children aged two and a half, three and a half and five and a half.

Fig. 5.8. Various emotions of children

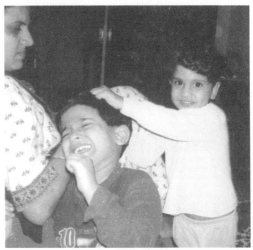

Fig. 5.9. Sibling rivalry

Although any emotion may be "heightened" in the sense that it occurs more frequently and more intensely than is normal for that particular individual, heightened emotionality in early childhood is characterized by temper tantrums, intense fears, and unreasonable outbursts of jealousy. Part of the intense emotionality of children at this age may be traced to fatigue due to strenuous and prolonged play, rebellion against taking naps and the fact that they may eat too little. Much of the heightened emotionality characteristic of this stage is psychological rather than physiological in origin. Most young children feel that they are capable of doing more than their parents will permit them to do and revolt against the restrictions placed upon them. In addition, they become angry when they find they are incapable of doing what they think they can do easily and successfully. Even more important, children whose parents expect them to measure up to unrealistically high standards will experience more emotional tension than children whose parents are more realistic in their expectations.

SOCIAL AND CULTURAL DEVELOPMENT

Early childhood is often called the pre-gang age. The foundations for socialization are laid as the number of contacts young children have with their peers increases with each passing year. Not only do they play more with other children but they also talk more with them.

Children between the ages of two and three years show great interest in watching other children and they attempt to make social contacts with them. This is known as parallel play. It is a play in which young children play independently beside other children rather than with them. If any contacts are made

Fig. 5.10. Social and cultural development

with other children, they tend to be frictional rather than cooperative. Parallel play is the earliest form of social activity young children have with their peers. Later, they engage themselves in associative play and in cooperative play.

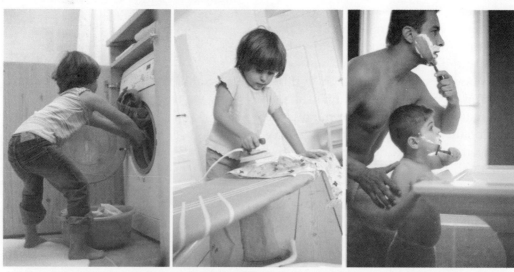

Fig. 5.11. Children imitating adults

The different forms of social behaviour are imitation, rivalry, cooperation, sympathy, empathy, social approval, sharing and attachment to people outside home such as a nursery teacher or to some inanimate object, such as a favourite toy or even a blanket. These then become what are known as attachment objects. For

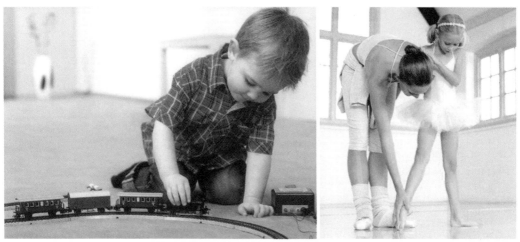

Fig. 5.12. Child's attachment to an object or a person

example, once a mother confided to me that her 2-year-old daughter has a favourite blanket and she sleeps with it always. Even if her mother is not with her, the blanket is enough for her.

Certain unsocial or antisocial behaviour patterns like negativism, aggressiveness, ascendant behaviours, selfishness, egocentrism, destructiveness, sex antagonism and prejudice are seen during this period. However, each of these apparently unsocial or antisocial patterns of behaviour is important as a learning experience that will enable young children to know what the social group approves and disapproves and what it will and will not tolerate.

Fig. 5.13. Children and cultural activities

During this period children show great interest in cultural activities like dramatization, singing and dancing.

SEXUAL DEVELOPMENT

During this stage in the developmental pattern, two important aspects of sex-role typing are expected to be mastered: learning how to play the appropriate sex role and accepting the fact that they must adopt and conform to the approved sex-role stereotype if they want to win favourable social judgments and in turn, social acceptance. Failure to do so will handicap children in their adjustment to the peer gangs that play such an important role in the social life of the older child.

Different children may learn sex-role stereotypes in different ways; the usual pattern is fairly predictable. They learn first that some children are girls and others are boys and some adults are women and some are men. At the same time they learn that they themselves are female or male. Then they learn that certain possessions - clothes, toys, books and play equipment are regarded as appropriate for one sex while others are associated with the other sex. They discover that certain personality characteristics and patterns of behaviour are associated with one sex while others are associated with the other sex. Gradually, they learn that males play certain roles in childhood as well as in adulthood while females play other roles. By the time early childhood draws to a close, most young children have fairly well developed sex-role stereotypes.

SPIRITUAL AND MORAL DEVELOPMENT

Fig. 5.14. Children praying during morning assembly

Children during this stage, develop spiritual and moral values through imitation. They follow their parents while praying in temples, churches, mosques, gurudwaras etc. Moral development in early childhood is on a low level. The reason is that they are not intellectually capable to learn or apply abstract principles of right and wrong. Neither do they have the necessary motivation to adhere to rules and regulations because they do not understand how these benefit them as well as members of the social group.

According to Piaget, early childhood is characterized by "Morality by constraint". In this stage of moral development, children obey rules automatically, without using reason or judgment and they regard adults in authority as omnipotent. They also judge all acts as right or wrong in terms of their consequences rather than in terms of the motivations behind them. According to the way young children view a matter, as wrong act results in punishment, which is dealt with either by other human beings or by natural or supernatural factors.

Kohlberg has elaborated on and extended Piaget's stages of moral development during early childhood to include two stages of this first level which he has labelled 'pre-conventional morality'. In the first stage, children are obedient and punishment oriented in the sense that they judge acts as right or wrong in terms of the physical consequences of these acts. In the second stage, children conform to social expectations in the hope of gaining rewards.

As early childhood comes to an end, habits of obedience should be established, provided children have had consistent discipline.

Discipline is society's way of teaching children the moral behaviour approved by the social group. Its goal is to let children know what behaviour is approved and what is disapproved and to motivate them to behave in accordance with these standards. In discipline, there are three essential elements. The first being the rules and laws which serve as guidelines for approved behaviour, the second is punishment for willful violation of the rules and laws and the third being the rewards for behaviour or attempts to behave in a socially approved way.

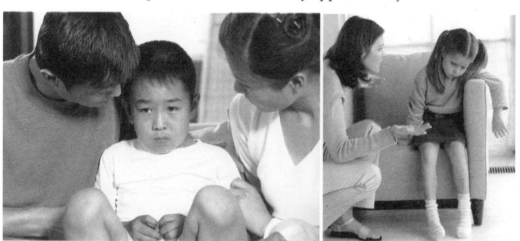

Fig. 5.15. Problem children being helped

During the early childhood years, major emphasis should be placed on the educational aspects of discipline and punishment should be given only when there is evidence that children not only know what is expected from them but when they willfully violate expectations. To increase young children's motivations to learn to behave in a socially approved manner, rewards serve the purpose of reinforcing the motivations.

Fig. 5.16. Enjoying a family meal   Fig. 5.17. Children enjoying a group activity

DEAR PARENTS, TEACHERS AND GUARDIANS

Early childhood can and should be a happy period in life and it is important for it to be so. Otherwise the habit of being unhappy can readily develop. Once the habit is developed , it will be hard to change. Parents and teachers have a daunting task

Fig. 5.18. An insecure child

to create a loving and accepting environment at home and at school for the children and this will have a positive influence on the child's life.

Happiness in early childhood depends partly on what happens to children such as the loss of a parent, friends and partly on conditions within themselves such as physical defects that prevent them from doing what their age-mates do or the failure to reach goals they set for themselves.

Two greatest causes for unhappiness in the 21st century children are : Psychological and physical rejection. Many children feel that they are not wanted and accepted by their parents.

The second greatest cause of unhappiness and emotional insecurity in children is the friction in the family and the breakup of the family. In each and every case of separation of parents, children are the victims. For example Gaurav, (Name changed) aged five from Montessori school was not regular in class. He always appeared sad and lethargic while all his companions were full of life and action. Alongwith this, he

Fig. 5.19. Children enjoying affection and acceptance

would faint in class. When fainting episodes were probed, it was found out that his parents were often in severe conflict and were in the process of legal separation.

It is thus the family's responsibility to see that their children have the four "A"s of happiness - Affection, Acceptance, Approval by others and Achievements which will encourage children to like and accept themselves.

Certain basic wants and needs of emotional security and economic security must be fulfilled if young children are to be happy.

Preparing to Welcome the New Member in the Family

Parents need to prepare the elder child in advance to welcome and accept the new arrival in the family. This can be done by the parents as well as by the grand parents. Let the elder child know that he/she is going to get one more companion and both of them are important to each other and for the parents. This will help the elder child to have a positive feeling towards the newcomer and the elder one will be at ease. When the gap between the first and second is three to four years, the acceptance becomes easier as compared to a long gap.

Some Characteristics of the Ordinal Position

The first borns try to behave in a mature way because they are expected to

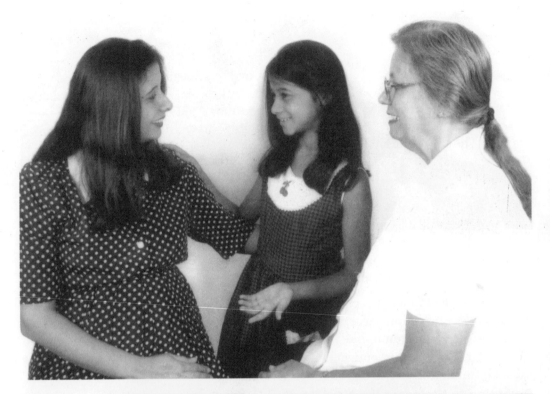

Fig. 5.20. Preparing to welcome the new member in the family

assume responsibilities. They resent to serve as models for the younger sibling and having to assume some of their care.

They may develop feelings of insecurity and resentment as a result of having been displaced from the centre of attention by a second born sibling. They develop leadership abilities as a result of having assumed responsibilities in the home. But these often lead to tendencies of being "bossy". They usually are high achievers or overachievers because of parental pressures and expectations and have a desire to win back parental approval if they feel that they are being replaced by younger siblings. They are often unhappy and jealous because of insecurity arising from

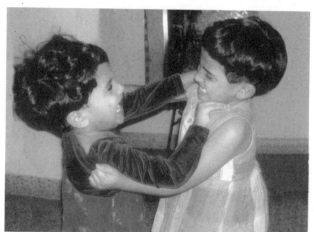

Fig. 5.21. Sibling Rivalry – Smita and Sheetal aged 3 and 4 making a point to each other. '*I am stronger than you*'

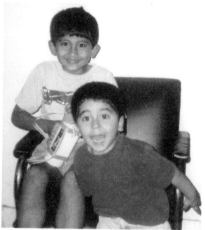

Fig. 5.22. Rohan and Roshan, aged 8 and 4, enjoying the company of each other

displacement by younger siblings and resentment at having more duties and responsibilities than younger siblings.

While middle borns try to compete with the first borns and the last borns in almost everything they learn to be independent and adventuresome as a result of greater freedom. They become resentful or try to emulate the other's behaviours when compared unfavourably with an older sibling. They become resentful and jealous when older and younger siblings are granted certain privileges. They act up and break rules in order to attract parental attention. They develop tendencies to 'boss', ridicule, tease, or even attack younger siblings who get more parental attention. They are plagued by feelings of parental neglect. This then encourages feelings of inadequacy and inferiority which in turn encourages development of behavioural disorders. They turn to outsiders for peer companionship.

On the other hand, the last borns tend to be happy because of attention and "spoiling" from family members during early childhood. They tend to be willful and demanding as a result of less strict discipline and "spoiling" by family members. Last borns have fewer resentments and greater feelings of security. They are usually protected by parents from physical or verbal attacks by older siblings and this encourages dependency and irresponsibility.

IS THE ONLY CHILD NORM — A LUXURY OR A BURDEN ?

From the point of view of parents, the only child norm may be a luxury, for whatever time and wealth they have, the only child will be the beneficiary. Parents may think of doing the best they can do for the child. The more the number of children, the more they think they will be burdened.

While on the other hand, the parents forget the fact that their only child has to face all their expectations by himself/ herself. This becomes a burden for the child and he/she will be a lonely victim without any other kith and kin with whom he/she can share his feelings freely.   The social development of an only child is also hampered since there are no

Fig. 5.23. A lonely boy !

opportunities for give and take as compared to other children who have brothers and sisters. In many cases the only child becomes self-centred and less social in his/her attitude and behaviour. Therefore, the only child is more burdened emotionally and socially if not economically.

GUIDANCE AT PRE-PRIMARY STAGE

(Age group $2\frac{1}{2}$ to 6 years)

This may be the first time the child is away from home to another place for three to four hours a day. This may be the first time that he is separated from his mother for so many hours. If he is prepared for it, he may accept it as a matter of course, but if not, he will refuse to have his mother out of sight and insist on her accompanying him and sitting with him.

Fig. 5.24. The 1st day in the school, away from parents can be a traumatic experience for a child

These early adjustments cause a lot of anxiety to parents. But nowadays, we see that major cities and towns have come up with many playschools which are like homes for babies of $2\frac{1}{2}$ to $3\frac{1}{2}$ years. Some of them are very good and sending children to some of these playschools will cost a fortune. The safety and security of many of the playschools should be properly checked before the children are sent. If the pre-primary class is small, in a home, in the next-door building, with lots of toys and young teachers who can sing and play and tell stories, the transition from home to school will not be difficult. But if it is located in a big school with hundreds of big children moving in and out, the infant gets totally lost and may refuse to go at all.

Pre-primary education is very important for sense-training, sense-perception and sense-discrimination. Parents need to be guided as to the school which is most suited according to the mental development and socio-economic group that the

Fig. 5.25. Children learn by observation

infant will have to encounter. If the atmosphere is friendly and happy, the infant will utilize the opportunity to the fullest and learn his first lessons of social behaviour and independence. If not, he will develop a tremendous dislike for any group interaction and his social adjustment will suffer. Most of the primary classes have now entrance tests for admitting the infant to make sure that he fits into their setting and is ready to be away from home. Parents mistake these for ability testing and drill infant into wrong perceptions and scare him such that instead of a pleasant experience at his class, he lands into dreadful fear and other maladjustment problems. Here is a real life experience as told by one of my students as she was travelling with her husband.

"On my way from Bangalore to Delhi on train, my husband and I were surprised to observe a peculiar yet interesting situation. A mother was taking her child to the bathroom every hour and in between she was drilling her with English alphabets and numbers. The child cried every time the mother took her to the bathroom. I asked her whether the child was unwell. She replied, "She is fine", and then continued, "Actually I've admitted her to X school (the name of the school is withheld) and I have heard that in case she has a problem of wetting the classroom, I'll have to pay a fine of Rs.50/- every time". I was sad at the plight of the child who was not willing to go to the bathroom and was crying". There are many similar cases where children ended up with treatment by doctors and child psychologists.

More than the infants, parents need guidance to help their infants face the first day at school and to choose the right school for them. Also, parents need to make sure that they do not hasten the infants' physical process. Unless the infant has had proper toilet-training, he is not ready for pre-primary education. Therefore, it is for parents to see whether their infants are physically and mentally ready for pre-primary education. If so, the school experience of children and parents will be a pleasant and fruitful one.

Here are few guidelines for teachers of pre-school though they may be familiar with them.

The children of pre-school (ages three years to five years) are too young physically and mentally to cope with the work of primary school. Their eye-movements, hand to eye co-ordination, muscles and bones are not mature enough to do the primary school work of reading and writing. But they are mature enough to start preparing for it.

Nursery training, Kindergarten training or Montessori training is therefore very important.

Activity must form an integral part of this period. He learns to sing, dance and play with others, learns to obey simple commands and follows directions. He gets used to being separated from his mother and learns to

Fig. 5.26. Children enjoy painting

adjust to a fixed schedule. Children at this age are very active, thus their motor skills can be developed through action songs, games that involve running, skipping and jumping. Their outdoor games as well as indoor activities should be always guided and supervised by the teachers. Otherwise, they may hurt themselves or hurt each other.

Children of early childhood have a very good rote memory. So they memorise short nursery rhymes, songs, short stories and small vocabularies with ease. They enjoy repetition and drill. Therefore, it is the best time to teach them various rhymes and correct vocabulary.

Children learn by imitation. They imitate the teachers rather their parents. Therefore, it is the responsibility of the teachers to teach them correct spelling and pronunciation and use correct language.

During the period of early childhood, the child is the centre of attention at home and most of the time he gets away with whatever he wants and demands. Now, the

Fig. 5.27. Children listening to a caring P.T. master

child has to change. He has to adjust with other children by sharing toys or by participating in various games. The child has to learn that he can't have his own way in everything. This change in his attitude is very important and this is nothing but informal education. Thus, teachers of Nursery, Kindergarten and Montessori schools

Fig. 5.28. Children enjoy action song

must be more interested in social and emotional development of the children rather than mere cognitive development.

SOME IMPORTANT FACTORS THAT CONTRIBUTE TO HAPPINESS IN EARLY CHILDHOOD

A loving family is a stimulating environment in which children have opportunities to use their abilities to the maximum and become well-balanced individuals later in life.

Good health in mind and body will enable young children to enjoy whatever they undertake and to carry it out successfully.

Parental acceptance of annoying childish behaviour and parental guidance in learning to behave in a socially more acceptable way lead children to be more self-confident and earn self-esteem.

Disciplinary policy that is well planned and consistently carried out by parents and teachers will let young children know what is expected of them and prevents them from feeling that they are unfairly punished.

Fig. 5.29. A loving and happy family

Reasonable and appropriate expressions of affection and recognition by parents and teachers such as showing pride in young children's achievements and spending time with them and doing things they want to do will make them appreciate themselves as well as others.

Encouragement of special ability, creativity and achievement in children, and avoiding ridicule or unnecessary criticism will help young children's enthusiasm to be creative and to be achievers and builders of home and society.

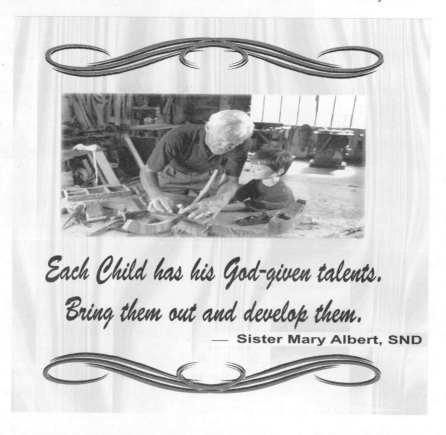

Each Child has his God-given talents.
Bring them out and develop them.

—— **Sister Mary Albert, SND**

CHILDREN AND CREATIVITY

Each child is a creator, so encourage her/his creativity.

Each child is an explorer, so encourage her/his need for exploration

Each child is an inventor so encourage her/his need for invention.

Fig. 5.30. Children in their creative best

The Almighty God is the creator of the universe. He has created us in His own image. We are elevated to be called as His creation. Therefore everyone of us ought to possess creative abilities. Each is a unique creation and each one has his unique ability which others may not have. Therefore the degree of possession of creative ability is not uniform. Some are found to possess high creative talents and they develop them to the fullest. These are the persons who move the world ahead by their discoveries and inventions in the field of science, art, literature, business, education and other fields of human accomplishments.

Fig. 5.31. Newton   Fig. 5.32. Albert Einstein and Rabindranath Tagore   Fig. 5.33. Michael Angelo

Newton, Thomas Edison, Albert Einstein, Rabindranath Tagore, Mahatma Gandhi, Abraham Lincoln, Shakespeare, Michael Angelo and Satyajit Ray were some of the creative individuals, who put their mark in their respective fields . Certainly, they were endowed with creative abilities, but the role of environment provided education, training and other various opportunities for creative expressions which helped them in nourishing and utilizing their creative abilities to the fullest.

According to Stagner and Karwoski, creativity implies the production of a totally or partially novel identity. While Skinner says, "Creative thinking means that the predictions and inferences for the individual are new, original, ingenious and unusual. The creative thinker is one who explores new areas and makes new observations, new predictions and new inferences"

Therefore, we can easily conclude that creativity is the capacity or the ability of an individual to create, discover or produce a new idea or object including the rearrangement or re-shaping of what is already known to him.

Some of the important characteristics of creative people are :

- **originality**
- **flexibility**
- **ideational fluency**
- **convergent and divergent thinking**
- **self-confidence**
- **self-reliance**
- **sensitiveness**
- **patience and persistence**
- **ability to see relationships and associations**
- **more adaptable and adventurous**
- **foresightedness**
- **intellectual curiosity and capacity to take independent decisions etc.**

Educational process, formal or informal should be aimed to develop creative abilities among children. The parents and teachers can either encourage or snub the creativity of children.

Teachers have that special power to inspire and motivate the child to bring out the creative genius in him. For example, let us listen to our ex-President Dr. APJ Abdul Kalam, what he said about his teacher.

"I was studying in Std. V, and must have been ten years of age. My teacher, Shri Siva Subramania Iyer was telling us how birds fly. He drew a diagram of a bird on the blackboard, depicting the wings, tail and the body with the head and then explained how birds soar to the sky. In the end of the class, I said I didn't understand. Then he asked the other students if they had understood, but nobody had understood how birds fly, he recalls."

Fig. 5.34. A.P.J. Abdul Kalam - ex-President of India - A creative genius

"That evening, the entire class was taken to the Rameshwaram shore, 'The ex-President continues, "My teacher showed us seabirds. We saw marvellous formations of them flying and how their wings flapped. Then my teacher asked us, 'Where is the bird's engine and how is it powered? I knew then birds are powered by their own life and motivation. I understood all about bird's dynamics. This was real teaching a theoretical lesson coupled with a live practical example. Shri Siva Subramani Iyer was a great teacher. That day my future was decided. My destiny was changed. I knew my future has to be about flight and flight systems; thus, my teacher was not only inspirational, but also enabled me to choose a career in aeronautics," he adds.

Creativity as a natural endowment, needs stimulation and nourishment. Most of the creative talents, if not given proper training, education and proper opportunities for creative expression will result in wastage.

Therefore, it becomes essential for the teachers as well as parents to realize the need for providing proper environment and creating conditions for full growth and development of the creative abilities of children.

Teachers can encourage creativity in children by the following ways:

● **Give freedom to respond and express in their own particular style. Remove all the fear and hesitation from children. Let them be as they are.**

● **Encourage originality, flexibility and fluency. Each one is unique and original in his own way. Each has his own way of solving a problem which is different from the other. So there is no single rigid or fixed formula to solve a problem. Encourage as many ideas, answers and solutions from children.**

● **Provide various opportunities for ego involvement so that she or he can say, 'It is my creation; or I have solved it'.**

Fig. 5.35. Children and their creative expression

● Provide them favourable atmosphere and appropriate opportunities for creative expression through curricular and extra curricular activities.

● Develop values and healthy habits in children. Truthfulness, hardwork, honesty, punctuality, self-reliance, self-confidence, love and brotherhood, patience and perseverence will help children to achieve their life's goal. Encourage healthy competition (competing with one's own previous record) and optimistic attitude in children. So that they can face any challenge and obstacle in life with courage and fortitude.

Fig. 5.36. Endurance till the end

- Relevant and flexible curriculum should be provided so that it would encourage the children's need for creativity, exploration, discovery and inventiveness.

- Use various techniques and methods, like, brainstorming, projects, creating models, debates, quiz programmes, cooperative learning, group discussions, independent study etc. for divergent thinking and new discoveries.

- Give examples and ideals of creative thinking. Parents and teachers must be role models of creative thinking in their life. They should believe in change, novelty, originality, and divergent thinking. Then and only then, they can inspire children to be creative.

WHAT IS CREATIVE THINKING?

Creative thinking is chiefly aimed to create something new. It is in search of new relationship and association to describe and interpret the nature of the things, events and situations. It is not bounded by any pre-established rules. The person himself usually formulates the problem and he is free to gather evidence and solution. The thinking of the scientists and inventors are examples of creative thinking.

Teachers and parents need to help children from their early life on for creative thinking. Don't discourage a child who is quite free and creative on his own. Sometimes the naughty and quiet ones who find the regular class quite boring may be the most creative and genius. So be patient with them and engage them in more challenging and independent work.

THE CREATIVE PROCESS OR STEPS IN CREATIVE THINKING

Creative thinkers are the inventors and discoverors of the world. A creative thinker like Thomas Edison left behind a wealth of inventions that leaves us all deeply in his debt. He invented the motion picture, the record player, and the light bulb. When he died, the United States of America as a nation switched off all electric lights for one minute in his memory, at a time decided on at the national level.

Creative thinkers follow some specific and definite steps. The steps (stages) emphasized by Munn, in his book "Introduction to Psychology" seem to be quite relevant. They are as follows :

(*a*) Preparation

(*b*) Incubation

(*c*) Inspiration or Illumination

(*d*) Verification or Revision

(a) Preparation

First, the problem is defined and analysed. Then all the relevant facts and materials considered essential for the solution are collected, and the plan of action is formulated. After this, one starts working according to the set plan. The work on the problem is continued. If need be, the plan of action is modified and the method of work be replaced by another method. If the work fails along the way, again many more datas and research material will be collected. In this way, continuous and persistant efforts are made. At some point, one finds that one cannot solve the problem. This frustration may lead to keep aside the work on the problem for the time being. But never given up, like Thomas Edison who marvelled at the bewildering total of his failures; 50,000 experiments, before he succeeded with the new storage battery.

(b) Incubation

The voluntary turning away from the problem is the beginning of the second stage – incubation. This time may be used for taking some rest, sleep or engaging in some other interesting activity. While doing this, some ideas interfering with the solution of the problem may fade away and a fresh new idea may suddenly surface as the solution to the problem.

(c) Inspiration or Illumination

This sudden appearance of an idea or insight to the solution of the problem is called as inspiration or illumination. Such inspiration may occur at any time, sometimes even while the thinker is sleeping or taking a walk.

(d) Verification or Revision

Once the thinker achieved the insight to the solving of the problem, he verifies the solution to the problem. This is called the final stage of verification. During this stage, the illumination or inspiration is tried out. He verifies to determine whether the solution or idea appeared through the insight is correct or not. In case it doesn't work well, fresh attempts are made for the solution of the problem. Sometimes the solution needs slight modification or change. Then in the light of the results of verification or testing, revision is made and the solution or idea is made quite workable. But at no stage, the creative thinker thinks it is completely perfect. It is always open for revision and essential modification at any time when needed.

The stages discussed above are not fixed as a creative thinker doesn't follow exactly as it is. Sometimes a creative thinker may experience an inspiration while he is on the first stage itself. Someone may not even get a solution after going through various stages for a long time. These given stages represent a scientific and systematic analysis of a higher creative process given by eminent creative thinkers.

A LETTER OF INTRODUCTION

Dear Teacher,

My son starts school today - it is all going to be strange and new to him for a while and I wish you would treat him gently. You see, uptill now, he has been the central attraction in our home. His mother has always been ready to repair his wounds and I have always been handy to soothe his feelings. But now, things are going to be different. This morning, he is going to walk down the front steps, wave his hands and start out on a great adventure.

Fig. 5.37. A loving father and son

It is an adventure that might take him across continents - it is an adventure that will probably include wars, tragedy and sorrow. To live this life in the world he has to live in, will require faith, love and courage. So, dear teacher, will you please take him by his hand and teach him things he will have to know. Teach him but gently, if you can. He will have to learn that all men are not just, that all men are not true. But teach him also that for every scoundrel, there is a hero - that for every crooked politician, there is a dedicated leader.

Teach him that for every enemy, there is a friend. It will take time, teacher, I know, but teach him if you can, that ten paise earned is of far more value than a rupee found. Teach him to learn how to gracefully lose - and enjoy winning - when he does win.

Steer him away from envy, if you can, and teach him the secret of quiet laughter. Let him learn early that bullies are the earliest people to lick. Teach him if you can, the wonder of books - but also give him time to ponder about the eternal mystery of birds in the sky, bees in the sun and the flowers on a green hill.

In school, teacher, teach him, it is far more honourable to fail than to cheat. Teach him to have faith in his own ideas, even if everyone tells him they are wrong. Teach him to be gentle with gentle people and tough with tough people.

Try to give my son the strength not to follow the crowd when everyone else is doing it - teach him to listen to everyone - but teach him also to filter all he hears on a screen of truth and take only the good that comes through. Teach him, if you can, how to laugh when he is sad - teach him there is no shame in tears – teach him there can be glory in failure and despair in success. Teach him to scoff at cynics.

Teach him to sell his talents and brains to the highest bidders, but never to put a price tag on his heart and soul. Teach him to close his ears to howling mob and stand and fight if he thinks he is right. Teach him gently, dear teacher, but don't spoil him because only test of fire makes fine steel.

Let him have the courage to be impatient - let him have the patience to be brave. Teach him always to have sublime faith in himself because then he will always have sublime faith in mankind and God.

This is a big order, teacher, but see if you can do–he is such a nice little boy - and he is my son.

DAD

CHAPTER **6**

Later Childhood

Fig.6.1. Group of children in later childhood

L ater childhood extends from the age of six years to the onset of puberty when the individual becomes sexually mature. Although it is possible to mark off the beginning of later childhood quite accurately, one can't be so precise about the time this period comes to an end because sexual maturity, the criterion used to divide childhood from adolescence, comes at varying ages. This is because there are marked variations in the ages at which boys and girls become sexually mature. There is also a difference between the children of Western countries and Indian children who achieve puberty earlier because of the favourable climatic and cultural factors. As a result, some children have a longer than average later childhood, while for others it is shorter than average. For the average American girl, the later childhood extends from six to thirteen, a span of seven years, for boys, it extends from six to fourteen, a span eight years, while for the average Indian girl later childhood extends from six to eleven years, a span of five years, for boys, six to thirteen years, a span of seven years.

According to the characteristics of this period, parents call later childhood as the troublesome age. There are many reasons for this. First of all they are no longer willing to do what they are told to do because they are more influenced by their peers than by their parents and other family members. Many older children, especially boys are careless and irresponsible about their clothes and other material possessions. Parents regard later childhood as the sloppy age generally because they don't care about their appearance and there is no order and neatness in their rooms. Even when there are strict family rules about grooming and taking care of possessions, few children of this age adhere to these rules unless parents demand and threaten them with punishment.

Later childhood is also regarded by many parents as the quarrelsome age since sibling rivalry is common. If the siblings in the family are of both sexes, it is common for the boys to pick on the girls, call names, ridicule them etc. When girls retaliate, quarrels ensue in which there are even physical attacks. In such cases the emotional climate of the home is far from pleasant for all family members.

While parents call later childhood the troublesome age, the psychologists regard it as the gang age. Their major concern is acceptance by their agemates and membership in a gang, especially a gang with prestige in the eyes of their agemates. Children are willing to conform to group approved standards in terms of appearance, speech and behaviour. This has also led psychologists to label later childhood as the age of conformity.

Educators call later childhood the elementary school age because it is the time when the child is expected to learn certain essential skills both curricular and extra-curricular. It is a critical period in the achievement drive. It is a time when children form the habit of being achievers, underachievers or overachievers.

Many factors that contribute to happiness in early childhood are equally important during the later childhood too. While happiness in later childhood does not guarantee lifetime happiness, the conditions that contribute to happiness will continue to do so as children grow older. This is especially true if the four "A"s of happiness — Affection, Acceptance, Approval and Achievement — are fulfilled.

During the later childhood period significant changes in the sphere of physical, intellectual, emotional and social aspects take place.

PHYSICAL DEVELOPMENT

Later childhood is a period of slow, steady and uniform growth until the changes of puberty begin. Development rate, although continuous and uniform, is very slow at this stage. Good and balanced diet is important for the child's good health, growth and development. The better the health and nutrition, the healthier the

Fig. 6.2. Organised physical exercise for children

children tend to be, age for age, as compared with those whose nutrition and health are poor.

INTELLECTUAL DEVELOPMENT

The rate of intellectual development is quite rapid at this stage which resembles the rate of physical growth at infancy. There is a rapid increase in understanding and in the accuracy of concept during later childhood, partly as a result of increased intelligence and partly as a result of increased learning experiences and opportunities. At this stage, the child acquires new experiences and tries to

Fig. 6.3. Children learn concepts

adapt himself to his environment and prepares himself to solve the problems. His power of reasoning, thinking, observation, concentration, perception, imagination etc., is developed. He cannot very well go with abstract thinking. He develops the concept of length, time and distance and learns to express himself in various ways. Areas of speech, pronunciation, vocabulary and sentence structure improve rapidly during late childhood, as does comprehension. In late childhood, the child's field of interests widens and he shows special aptitudes, likings and dislikings towards things and work. Children of this age are usually extroverts and are very fond of excursions and visits. They develop interest in reading various types of books. Radio, television, drama and movies hold a strong appeal for them. They are interested in everything that is mysterious and romantic. Wide differences in the interest pattern can be seen among boys and girls. Boys are interested in activities requiring fearlessness, courage and adventures while girls are inclined towards the activities requiring feminine characteristics.

They develop a realistic attitude. They begin to accept and appreciate the hard realities of life. They no longer believe in fairy tales but believe in reality and try to adapt themselves to the real environment.

EMOTIONAL DEVELOPMENT

It is a period of emotional stability and control. Children learn to control the overt expressions of their emotions. The child now hides his feelings. He can control his emotions and express them in appropriate and socially approved ways. His emotional behaviour is not guided by instinctive causes but has an appropriate rationale behind it.

SOCIAL DEVELOPMENT

This period of childhood is often called gang age because they are always interested in activities with their peers and want to be members of a gang and they have a strong sentiment for the group. Feelings of mutual cooperation, teamspirit and

Fig. 6. 4. Children and peer group activities

group loyalties are developed among the children of their age. As gang members, children often reject parental standards, develop an antagonistic attitude towards members of the opposite sex and become prejudiced against all who are non gang members.

SEXUAL DEVELOPMENT

Sexual development at this stage is called 'latency period'. Sexual energy at this stage generally remains dormant but emerges with great force at the end of this stage. Older children want to know more details about the relations between the sexes, the father's role in reproduction, and the birth process. They try to get such information from books or from their friends with whom they exchange 'dirty' stories and jokes. Children at this stage develop an attitude of antagonism and indifference towards the opposite sex. Children at this stage like to play with the members of their own sex. Sex antagonism is more pronounced in boys than in the case of girls. They do not want anything that resembles a girl. While girls show indifference to boys and tease and interfere with their play.

RELIGIOUS AND MORAL DEVELOPMENT

Discipline plays an important role in the development of moral code. Children at this stage still follow religious exercises like prayer, going to the temple, church,

Fig. 6.5. Children and religious development

mosque etc. Various sentiments like religious, moral, social and patriotic begin to develop at this stage. They pick up many social virtues at this stage since they follow the group spirit. Thus the type of group and values held by the group have a greater influence on the children.

Fig. 6.6. Children recalling the sacrifices of freedom fighters

SOME PROMINENT BEHAVIOURAL DISORDERS IN THE PRIMARY SCHOOL CHILDREN

Bedwetting : Nervous, rejected, frustrated and emotionally insecure children of this age group start bedwetting. It is a common disorder in boys as compared to girls.

Fig. 6.7. Problem children

The main causes for this problem may be from family or from the school environment.

If a child of school age still wets his bed, parents and teachers need to probe for an explanation. Was learning to keep dry overemphasized from the beginning? Did he really learn to keep dry? Is the wetting of a fairly recent appearance? What events in his life may be tied up to it? Did something occur that was a threat to him? For example, the arrival of a new baby which has caused divided attention given to him now. Did he bring poor marks in the exams? Did he have to give up a room, a bed, or a chair which was meant just for himself? Was he punished for sex play with other children? In short, is this his way of getting attention?

If he wets the bed often for a long time, in all probability he has a chronic condition and needs medical help. If he is medically fit, then the cause may be psychological. He may be feeling rejected, unwanted or emotionally insecure because there is continuous fight between parents and he is the victim. Or the parents may be divorced. Is he the dull one in a bright family?

Is he under strain because he has just entered the regular school with long hours and with more subjects to study? Is he finding it difficult to adjust with the new teachers and classmates? Is the new school environment rather difficult as compared to the playschool where he had less time to spend and less work to do? Most important of all, is he made to feel miserably ashamed of his habit? Is he punished, scolded or ridiculed in front of others?

Once a child becomes fearful of not being able to stay dry, his anxiety piles up. He becomes afraid and embarrassed. As parents and teachers, what we can do for a child who has bed wetting trouble, is to try to take whatever load he is carrying off his shoulders. If there is high academic expectation from the parents, then the parents need to understand his abilities and weaknesses and accept him as he is. All efforts must be made to make him feel loved, accepted, comfortable, and light hearted. If we discover he is emotionally excitable, things that overstimulate him must be avoided. He needs occupations and interests that will encourage concentration.

Practical ways that help him overcome this habit can also be taught. For example, having an alarm clock in his room that will awaken him at a particular time (bed-wetters are usually very deep sleepers). In most cases, a **CHANGE OF PARENTS' ATTITUDES** and their love and acceptance will make it no longer necessary for the child to return to the helplessness of babyhood.

Fig. 6.8. Nail biting

Fig. 6.9. Thumb sucking

The other behavioural disorders are thumb sucking, nail-biting, temper tantrums, bragging, teasing, cruelty, timidity and the aggressive ones may start stealing, lying, cheating, fighting with siblings, breaking possessions of other family members, neglecting home responsibilities, being rude to adult family members, being sneaky, spilling things intentionally, destroying school property, annoying other children by teasing them, bullying them and creating disturbance, reading comic books or chewing gum during school hours, fighting with classmates and playing truancy.

Thus adjusting to the school environment, class pressures, scholastic work and artificial surroundings are not easy for the six-year-old. Some children cannot withstand all these tensions and show behavioural disorders.

Only guidance can help them to return to normality. Both, the parents and the teacher need guidance so that they can understand the child better and assist him/her to make adjustments in his/her life.

SOME LEARNING DIFFICULTIES AND SPEECH HAZARDS

Some learning difficulties are in the areas of visual skills in reading, auditory skills in reading comprehension, spelling skills, arithmetic and computational skills and problem solving skills.

Speech hazards are :

Children with vocabulary handicaps in their school work as well as in their communication with others are seen during this stage. Speech errors, such as mispronunciations and grammatical mistakes and speech defects, such as stuttering or lisping are the other defects. These children become so self-conscious that they will speak only when necessary. Children who have difficulty in speaking the language used in their school environment may be handicapped in their efforts to communicate and may be made to feel that they are "different". Egocentric speech, critical and derogatory comments, and boasting are some unpleasant characteristics found in some children during this stage. These behaviours may antagonize their peers.

GUIDANCE AT THE PRIMARY SCHOOL STAGE
(Age Six To Nine)

In the first place, guidance is needed for parents to find out appropriate schools according to the family's economic standard, for good schools charge exorbitant fees. Guidance is also needed to find out which school maintains a good scholastic standard and provides a number of co-curricular activities. Good schools maintain highly qualified staff. The medium of instruction and locality of the school are equally important. It is also necessary to know which socio-economic class of pupils is catered to.

As for the child, this is the first step to formal education and he finds himself in a totally new and different environment than the one he was used to in the pre-primary stage. He had a friendly, homely and a pleasant environment and now suddenly he finds himself in a crowded classroom with strangers all around. He finds it difficult to adjust with 60 or 65 children in a classroom with very uncomfortable seats for six or seven hours a day. In some cases, there is hardly any space to move around; the classrooms may be dark and dingy, the benches broken and rickety and the surrounding may be dirty too. This is an artificial situation for the child. He loves to move about and play, be outdoors and stretch himself.

Along with long hours in the school (9 a.m. to 4 p.m. or 8 a.m. to 3 p.m.) the child has to learn more subjects like languages, mathematics, science, social sciences, art and craft, music, dance, P.T., etc. These days in many cases, children attend various other extra-curricular activities after school hours like swimming, dance, music, sports and in some cases, tuition too. This is an entirely new situation for the six-year-old child with lots of pressure. He also finds it difficult to adjust with the new teachers and their methods of instructions. In certain cases, if a child asks any question, he may be snubbed by the teacher or ridiculed by his classmates. He can't talk to his friends, for then, he would be referred to as undisciplined and he dare not get up from his seat, for he may be given punishment. Some disciplinary measures given by the teacher have a negative influence on the child.

Primary school teachers have a great role in the educational and personal development of children. Primary school children have great regard and respect for their teachers. For them, teachers are always correct and they believe in whatever the teacher says or does. Therefore, it is the responsibility of the teacher to set a good example in every way.

Children between the ages of six and nine have a very short span of attention. Their abstract thinking is not yet developed, the concept of time, space, length, weight etc. are crude, their muscle coordination is still imperfect and yet they are very active because of their muscle development. Therefore their learning material and the class timings should be shorter. Learning materials should be attractive and colourful. Since their abstract thinking is not developed, concrete objects and a variety of teaching aids should be used to make the concept clear. Teachers must not over emphasise on reading or writing. Handwriting can't be expected to be good. If over emphasised, it'll have a negative influence on the children's reading and writing. But the teacher can help the child to improve his/her handwriting.

Fig. 6.10. Individual attention by the teacher is always a big booster for any child

A true educator must
cultivate a personality,
which manifests kindness and patience.

— Sister Mary Elsedia, SND

This is the time when children who cannot cope up with the schoolwork are identified, for example, the mentally retarded are referred to special schools where they can pick up some craft, instead of wasting time in a normal school. The slow learners or scholastically backward, who may have personality problems result in poor scholastic performance, can also be placed in schools for slow learners. If these children are referred early to the child-guidance clinics, they can be saved from permanent damage to their development.

At this stage, diagnostic and remedial instructions are helpful for children who consistently show poor performance in a certain subject. These children can be given special coaching classes or sent to catch-up clinics or to remedial teaching classes. This will help them to come up to the expected level of achievement. Thus we see that children in the primary level face a number of psychological and educational problems and only an effective guidance programme can solve them and help the children in adjusting to themselves, to others and to circumstances.

Thus adjusting to school environment, class pressures, scholastic work and artificial surroundings are not easy for the six-year-old. Some children cannot withstand all these tensions and show behavioural disorders.

DIAGNOSTIC AND REMEDIAL INSTRUCTIONS

When the children are in the second half of the 3rd standard, the teacher needs to start the Diagnostic and Remedial Instructions. If it is not done at this stage, then when the children are at the beginning of 4th standard, diagnostic and remedial instructions should be started without any delay. This is meant for the children who show learning difficulties in their education.

What is Educational Diagnosis?

Educational Diagnosis deals with the breakdown or failure of a child in the process of education. The breakdown may be due to the blockage in the learning process of a child caused either by the child himself, a situation or the teacher. The main purpose of educational diagnosis is to locate the nature and root cause of learning difficulties and deficiencies and suggest remedies for the removal of these blockages from the child's education process.

What are the aims of Educational Diagnosis?

For Gandhiji, "It is through education, we are going to develop head, heart and hand."

The aims of education have become three-fold, the aims of educational diagnosis are also three-fold. That is, it covers corrective measures, preventive measures and enrichment programmes.

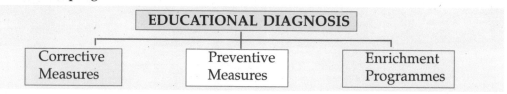

EDUCATIONAL DIAGNOSIS		
Corrective Measures	Preventive Measures	Enrichment Programmes

Corrective Measures : It is noticed that a child not only faces problems in academic field but also in other fields in his life. In fact, it is like a vicious circle which influences each other. When we probe deep into the reason for the child's lack of interest and achievement in academic field, we may investigate the causes of the child's emotional disturbances, their cause may be due to home atmosphere or his teacher in the school, but whatever may be the reason, it leads to the failure in his academic field and causes economic wastage and wastage of time. A child who has otherwise intellectual capabilities, should be given proper guidance to overcome all these difficulties. The symptoms will be compared with other similar causes and the corrective measure should be suggested so that the child can improve his way of learning.

Preventive Measures : Educational diagnosis refers to the prevention of learning difficulties which occur in children. As blockage may be due to various reasons, preventive measures can be taken to avoid the repetition of the mistakes. If the blockage is caused by the teacher, the teacher can prevent many drawbacks in his teaching which act as blockages in the learning process of children. He can modify his teaching methods and select one which is most suitable for the child. But if the blockage is caused by economic circumstances, social background, family environment, atmosphere in the neighbourhood or any other emotional reasons, the root cause of the blockage should be detected and pinpointed and proper measures should be taken to prevent further occurrence of the situation.

Enrichment Programmes: Educational diagnosis does not stop at the corrective measures and prevention of the causes of the different mistakes but emphasizes on the enrichment programme. In fact, remedy and enrichment are two sides of the same coin. In both we have to study the student in relation to his inherent capacities and intellectual abilities. If he is an underachiever, he needs a remedial programme to bring him upto the expected level. If he has already crossed his level, he is only in need of some enrichment programme to excel himself. So, the aim of both is improvement of achievement, though the methods may be different.

Fig. 6.11. Children at enrichment programme

To conclude, we can say educational diagnosis in modern times aims at the remedy and enrichment of all aspects, i.e., cognitive, conative and affective aspects. Apart from the social values, personality development is taken into consideration. Enrichment programmes help to cultivate in a child all these aspects and every teacher plays an important role to find out the child's difficulties at an early stage. In the early stage, the removal of the blockage is much easier without any further development of breakdown or blocking in the learning process.

Need for Educational Diagnosis

The need for educational diagnosis arose when different educational problems led to the wastage and stagnation at all stages of education. Wastage refers to the economic wastage that is a material loss.

Wastage : It takes place when a percentage of students enter a particular stage of education and fail to complete it. It includes dropouts, failing in one class for a number of times, leaving the studies etc. It is noticed that in many schools especially in rural areas, the students after studying up to 5th or 6th standard leave school. The reasons may be numerous but this ultimately causes the economic and social loss of our country.

Stagnation : This refers to the situation when the child has to repeat the same experience of a certain standard which he fails to complete successfully, for example, if a student fails in one standard, the general tendency is then to force him to repeat the same class for another year, so that he can produce better result. In this case, the authority is totally oblivious about various reasons that caused the student's failure. However, stagnation is more prevailing in the government-aided schools. Since government is providing the finance for educating them, repetition of the same class causes economic wastage for our nation as well as wastage of time for the student.

The various purposes of remedial teaching programmes are : reconditioning habit and skill, correcting errors in knowledge, improving personality traits, resolving conflicts, substituting good attitudes, interests and ideals in the place of undesirable ones, treating serious defects of pupils in physical, social and emotional areas and curing educational ills by preventive measures. For the counsellor, the remedial teaching programme does not mean handling the learning disability but the learner himself and his personality.

Moreover, the need for educational diagnosis is felt because it gives a feedback to the teacher to plan necessary activities for the child which helps in the continuous process of development of a child.

What is learning? What is wrong learning?

By learning, we mean a change in behaviour. To be more precise and perfect we can say that learning refers to a more or less permanent change in behaviour through experience.

What is wrong learning?

Learning takes place by establishing a bond between the stimulus and the response. When a wrong response is connected or associated with a stimulus, it is wrong learning. For example, a strange person enters the room, at the same moment the child hears a thundering sound and he gets frightened. Now the child associates the person with a frightening sound and whenever he comes he feels frightened.

Here we find that the child has established a wrong bond between the stimulus and response. This is wrong learning.

There are many factors that disturb the child's learning and unknowingly the child establishes wrong bonds while learning. These wrong bonds interfere in his learning which result in learning difficulties.

Some of the factors that contribute to learning difficulties are of a permanent kind, others are temporary in character and can easily be avoided or prevented.

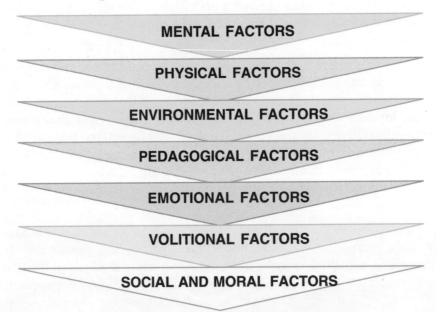

MENTAL FACTORS

PHYSICAL FACTORS

ENVIRONMENTAL FACTORS

PEDAGOGICAL FACTORS

EMOTIONAL FACTORS

VOLITIONAL FACTORS

SOCIAL AND MORAL FACTORS

Fig. 6.12. Factors which block learning in children

Mental Factors: Lack of native intelligence may lead to failure or to make satisfactory progress in the school work. Therefore, when making a diagnosis of the slow progress of a child it is essential to judge the mental level of the pupil. This may be determined by a standard intelligence test. However, the level of mental ability may be the only factor to be considered. It has been found that pupils markedly deficient in arithmetic have a range of 75 to 135 which show that pupils of relatively high mental ability may encounter serious difficulties in some subject, owing to other factors which must be determined by systematic enquiry.

Physical Factors : Many pupils fail to make satisfactory progress due to various physical defects, such as defects in vision or hearing. The pupils may be undernourished, anaemic or fatigued. Due to previous serious illness, their health may be undermined and hence they are not able to make sustained efforts required for successful school work. Many students have been labelled as stupid or have been thought by their teacher to be inattentive when as a matter of fact they could neither see nor hear what was being written or said in the class.

Environmental Factors: A congenial environment at home is essential for learning while a negative environment causes blockage in learning. If the family environment is full of friction, the child finds it difficult to learn. Conflict between parents, broken homes, divorced or separated parents make the school going children anxious in their lives. The unhealthy environment at home makes the children difficult to concentrate in their studies.

The uneducated parents and the lack of motivation in the parents also become poor environmental factors for learning.

Therefore, a healthy environment is an essential factor for better learning in children.

Fig. 6.13. Children who face an unhealthy environment develop lack of confidence

Pedagogical Factors : Deficiencies in the pupils work is due to factors over which the school has control. These factors may be due to the following :

(a) First, inadequacy of reference books and notes based on syllabus. The curriculum may not have been scientifically constructed. In the syllabus little attention instead of a thorough attention may be given to the probable learning difficulties while presenting a subject. Hence in the initial presentation of a topic, textbooks may plunge the pupils at once into a state where many difficult points have occurred which have not been previously presented and consequently the pupils fail to master the subjects. The textbooks may be uninteresting and unattractive and difficult for the pupils.

(b) Second, mass approach of teaching gives little consideration to individual needs. Consequently, the pupils through trial and error during undirected practice may acquire faulty work habits and round about inefficient method of work and this seriously interferes with the efficiency of his performance. For example, the pupil fails to do long divisions due to weakness in subtraction, which is an important step in division. The child fails to understand the content of the text because of faulty reading habits and poor comprehension.

(c) Continuous absence of pupils causes serious gaps in learning a subject. For example, maths being a very sequential subject, students remain weak because of these gaps.

(d) Transfer of pupils from one school to another school often results in serious gaps due to differences in method, approach and curriculum.

Emotional Factors: Emotional disturbances often have an important relation to pupil's failure in school work. Fear of teacher or principal may inhibit his responses to a marked degree. Hatred towards a teacher is transferred to the subject that he/she teaches. Some pupils feel keenly the unpleasantness that arises in the activities of daily life. Some students develop antisocial tendencies which result in lying, cheating, malingering. Improper handling by the teacher, bad companions, uncongenial atmosphere at home for learning, conflicts between parents always disturb the pupils emotionally and thus cause blockage in learning.

A healthy social and personal relationship between teachers and pupils is vital for effective learning. If a teacher has a strong, rich and sympathetic personality and uses a clinical approach to deal with pupils, he can definitely help children to do away with their problems.

Study of pupil's likes and dislikes, their interest in play, their relations with the classmates, their reaction to praise and reproof, will help the teacher to plan the curricular activities. Constructive measures should be taken to develop a strong positive attitude towards school work and to eliminate all factors that may tend to develop negative reactions.

Sympathetic conferences with parents of problem cases can help to bring about improvement in home conditions. A favourable home environment with a strong emotional support by parents help the children to learn better.

Volitional Factors : Some pupils fail to progress because of lack of effort on their part. It may be due to lack of interest or sheer laziness or lack of confidence in their ability to master the topic.

Such pupils are often unwilling to ask the teacher for assistance, as a consequence flounder helplessly. They are shy and different. They fail to stick to the task until it is finished. To avoid volitional weaknesses the teacher should create interesting situations in which the pupil will be impelled to active learning through the urge from within. Through charts, progress cards, self-motivation graphs, merit schemes, the teacher may stimulate the students to activity and for self-improvement and growth. Develop a right type of relation between the teacher and the pupil, with the teacher as a guide and counsellor and not as a task master.

Social Factors : Faulty attitude of pupils have their roots in unsatisfactory environmental conditions. Indifference of parents to pupils' success in daily classroom situations or unnecessary nagging at home and in the school work may worsen the situation. One of the main aims of school is to provide a proper social environment in which (school society in miniature) undesirable and antisocial traits will be nipped in the bud and worthwhile qualities will be developed. Socialized forms of school work such as group discussion, projects, group activities and co-operative learning are effective methods for better learning.

Moral Factors : In making a diagnosis of the child's difficulties, some consideration must be given to the moral qualities of an individual.

Moral qualities like love, peace, trust, honesty, hard work, justice, sharing, equality, respect, dignity, and so on help develop in the student deeper sense of personal integrity and social worth.

Conformity to the social norms and adapting to the various situations in the environment will lead the student to achieve success in life.

Most of the causes internal to the student may however be located in the area of scholastic aptitude, retardation of basic skills, work study habits, physical factors and emotional factors.

Remedy : After understanding the cause for the student's learning difficulty, we come to the stage of applying remedial measures.

Remedial Teaching Programmes

The educational guidance programme necessitates the service of providing remedial teaching programmes for those individual students who have registered errors in learning and which have been detected by diagnostic tests.

1. Remedy Should be Accompanied by Strong Motivational Programmes

The importance of motivation cannot be over emphasized. No remedial measures can succeed unless the students are duly motivated to take them. The purposes of the measures should be related to the needs of the students who should feel convinced of their utility. Students should take up the remedial activity willingly. The old saying "We can take the horse to water but we cannot make it drink it". Drink works well here also. The students should be made to feel the thirst for remedy.

2. Begin Where the Pupil is

One of the greatest mistakes made in all phases of teaching is in assuming that a pupil knows more than what he really does. New material or advanced work cannot be successfully introduced with the pupil unless he has developed a readiness for it.

3. Remedy Should be Individualized in Terms of Psychology of Learning

Students motivation is inter related with individualization of remedy. Remedial measures given on individual basis by considering their needs and requirements and bend of mind will no doubt be more effective. But this need should not be stretched too far because it is neither very necessary nor practical to individualize remedy in all cases. There will always be students having similar difficulties caused by such factors which can be taken care of collectively at least in scholastic field. Such students can be conveniently grouped together for remedy. For example, framing grammatically incorrect sentences and using wrong spellings are commonly found with regard to English. Such students could be provided remedy collectively.

4. Continuity of Evaluation and Informing the Pupil Frequently About his Progress

Remedy does not end the moment the remedial activity is given to the pupil. In fact it is the beginning. First, steps should be taken to find out at each activity as to how far they have succeeded. Remedy itself should be continually evaluated because as it proceeds new problems, new difficulties and new needs may arise necessitating a rethinking. The remedial programme should be modified to meet the demands of the situation.

Second, making the child aware about his progress is an important aspect of remedy. By means of charts, graphs and records, the improvement made by the child should be clearly shown. This pictorial display of the improvement provides a powerful spur to learning.

5. Abundant and Varied Exercises and Activities

Abundant and varied exercises and activities should be provided. The success of the remedial programmes depends upon how far the teacher has helped the child to sustain interest in it. For this, drill and repetition should be used. Repetition and drill should be varied, otherwise they create monotony in the work done by the pupils.

6. Definite Satisfaction on the Part of the Pupils Should Accompany the Work

At each little achievement the child's efforts should be recognized. A pat on the back, a good word of praise or recognition by the teacher would work miracles in case of children. "Practice which renders satisfaction to the child accounts for rapid learning", according to Thorndike. A good effect of learning may provide extra motivation to the child to continue with the remedial exercise.

Remedial programmes may not always need a separate time allocation for them. But they will always mean some extra work for both the teacher and the students who are affected. In difficult cases some extra time may also be required. In most of the cases an ingenious teacher can take care of most of it along with his regular teaching. A little more attention to under achievers keeping in mind their weakness during classwork will do the trick. Remedial teaching is not some different type of teaching, it is just good teaching.

Fig. 6.14. Remedial teaching : Young student being guided by the teacher

We may conclude with the definition of Remedy given by (Glenn Myers Blair) Dr. D.G.M. Blair which has all aspects of remediation appropriately.

"Remedial teaching is essentially good teaching which takes the pupils at his own level and intrinsic methods of motivation leads him to increased standard of competence. It is based upon a careful diagnosis of the defects and is geared to the needs and interest of pupils."

GUIDANCE AND COUNSELLING IN MIDDLE SCHOOL STAGE
(Age group between 9 yrs to 12 years)

At this stage, the same subjects are taught as in the primary for all individuals, irrespective of differences in abilities and interests. The problems faced by students are of a different nature. First of all, they are used to a single teacher (class teacher) for almost all the subjects except for one or the other. Suddenly they find themselves having separate teachers for seperate subjects. Adjustment to various teachers is a big problem. Adjustment to the teaching methods from one teacher to another teacher is a problem and the young child gets confused.

The classwork as well as homework increases with a large number of teachers, and subjects, for they do not coordinate among themselves and insist on their own work to be completed. Moreover, the child's learning method needs to be different in the upper primary. He has to gradually wear out his rote learning method to judicious learning or learning with comprehension.

A good guidance programme providing information about how to comprehend, how to study, how to think, how to memorise, in short, how to develop healthy study habits is very important at this stage. Regular study habits can pave the way for future scholarly habits and need to be emphasized at this stage to help the child keep away from learning by bits and parts.

This stage needs Diagnostic and Remedial Instructions. (Refer the Diagnostic and Remedial Instructions). This includes taking care of the weak students by paying more attention to them and by providing special coaching classes or by giving remedial programmes. The Average, Good and Very Good students have to be provided an academically stimulating environment. The underachievers should be detected and brought to the expected level by appropriate programmes. The gifted children will find the normal classes quite boring. Therefore the gifted children should be provided with challenging and extra activities. Mentally stimulating activities will keep them occupied and they will be benefited much for their development. If they are not given more challenging and independent work, they may become maladjusted and frustrated children. Gifted children have few special needs like the need for knowledge and understanding. They have a need for creativity, need for development of their exceptional abilites, need for self-actualization and self-expression. Besides their basic needs, if these special needs are not satisfied, the gifted children may be emotionally and mentally disturbed.

Fig. 6.15. Talent awareness during morning assembly in the school

This stage sees a very rapid mental and physical development of the child and therefore, maximum number of curricular and co-curricular activities need to be provided. A good guidance worker can assess the intelligence as well as interests of the pupils and provide such programmes which would maximize their potential.

Fig. 6.16. Encourage talents in children

Since physical development is continuous and the intellectual development is quite rapid, provide them with worthwhile mental and physical activities like girls joining Guides and boys joining Cubs and Scouts.

During this stage, few girls may reach puberty and they'll have their menstrual periods. This may be a great shock to the young girls who are just 10, 11 or 12 years old. Even some parents will be surprised to see this. Therefore, both the parents and teachers need to be prepared to take care of such cases with understanding and care.

Hence, even at the middle school level though instruction is uniform, individuals show marked differences and guidance is necessary for healthy growth and development. The search for development of talent is a continuous process and should begin at this stage for the benefit of those who stand out in their groups in scholastic as well as other co-curricular and physical activities like sports and games. Once explored the teachers need to be guided to provide individual attention and atmosphere for free expression and creative work for such talented ones.

There may be about five percent of the pupils who may show behavioural disorders and need to be specially guided. Some of the behavioural problems of the primary level may be carried to the middle school level if they were not detected there and corrected. Some boys may still continue with the problem of bedwetting. This has to be corrected through proper guidance and counselling programmes. The other problems may be fighting with the siblings at home, lying, cheating, stealing, bullying, using vulgar and obscene language, fighting with the classmates, playing truant etc.

In some cases very strict parents are the cause for their children's lying and cheating. They expect their children to be perfect in everything they do. Many parents have high expectations about the quality of their children's schoolwork

You can't use the same method everytime, they work on the first occasion and fail on the next hundred. You have to vary them.

— St. Julie Billiart

and the amount of responsibility they will assume in the home. When children fail to meet these expectations, parents often criticize, nag and punish. In order to avoid such punishment and to please their parents, some of them give a wrong report about their result or even change the marks in the reportcard. (For example, the actual marks in Maths would have been 55, but the student changes it to make it appear as 85.

In the case of an only child, the expectations from the parents are even higher and he/she will become a single victim of parental high expectations.

The following letter of a student is a true example to illustrate the above:

I did not realise at first that I would get caught. And I was caught and I told lies and went home I could not concentrate on whatever I was doing. I wanted to come and tell that I had lied but here again. I was frightened because I thought my parents would be called and spoken. As I am very very scared of my parents. They expect me to be perfect in what ever I do but which I am unable to keep up. So because of this I had to tell lies.

But now I have learnt to accept my wrong doings and from that day I have come to realise that by telling the truth I have found much more peace and also happiness. If this incident had not taken place I would have surely continued to say lies and be

be lazy about doing anything.
Through this experience I have
gained courage to tell the truth.
I started telling lies when
I was in the 7th Std. Because during
this year I was unable to study in
this class as I found certain subjects
hard. So the first type of lies I
said was that the teacher did not
teach well etc. I feel that I tell
lies only due to the fear that my
parents are strict with me. If I was
wrong they never sit and reason why
I was wrong but spank me and shout
at me.

Anyway now I know that things
work in a better way if I speak
the truth and I have also found to
my surprise that I feel a lot of peace
within me.

I am very sorry about what
happened but I am also happy about
what happened because if something
like this had not taken place I
would have never realized the
happiness of being truthful.

> **Teachers have the power to affect a child's life for better or for worse. A child becomes what he experiences.**

MOTIVATE YOUR CHILD TO LEARN

Thomas Edison, one of the greatest inventors of the world was an intrinsically motivated person. He never completed his formal schooling. He could never get along with his teachers and other students. So he discontinued his studies. He had only four years of formal schooling. But he taught himself to read physics and chemistry books and the Bible. He set up a small laboratory at home. He faced plenty of financial problems, yet he never gave up. He continued to carry out thousands of experiments. He became one of the best scientists due to his self-motivation.

A friend of Thomas Edison asked him about the result of his experiments. Thomas Edison exclaimed, marvelling at the bewildering total of his failures – 50, 000 experiments, for example, before he succeeded with the new storage battery; "Results", he said, " Why man, I have gotten lots of results; I know 50,000 things that won't work."

Motivation is an inner urge to do something or to achieve something. The individual, keeps on trying till he achieves his goal. The mind, heart, hand and the whole person is involved when one is motivated to achieve something. He never gives up till he achieves it. A boy who learns cycling loses balance and falls during the initial time but he never gives up, till he learns it. Take for example, the atheletes of world ranking. Their self-motivation, helped in their perseverence and they achieved what they wanted in their respective field.

According to Kelly "motivation is the central factor in the effective management of the process of learning. Some type of motivation must be present in all learning."

Motivation is classified into intrinsic motivation or self-motivation and extrinsic motivation or artificial motivation.

Intrinsic motivation or self-motivation is the mental determination and will to achieve what the individual wants. Intrinsically motivated persons determine the goals and act strongly to achieve them. The individual finds interest within the activity and he derives pleasure from doing it, just like Thomas Edison who kept on doing the experiments and enjoyed doing them. While in the extrinsic motivation, the individual does the work in order to get an external reward. For example, some children study very hard in order to get a reward from the parents.

Intrinsic motivation or self-motivation, as a source of spontaneous inspiration and stimulation brings better results, especially in the field of teaching and learning process. Therefore, it is always better to make use of the intrinsic or self-motivation.

Intrinsic motivation or self-motivation can be cultivated through believing in oneself.

"They are able because they think they are able", said 'Virgil.'

- Through resolute self-confidence.
- Making a list of goals in one's life and arranging them in the order of priority and setting a date to reach them.
- Listing the steps one must take to reach one's goals.
- Listing the qualities one needs to achieve them.
- Identifying the qualities one lacks to achieve these goals.
- A very positive attitude and approach in life.
- Overcoming the negative qualities through constructive means. Totally focussed and committed to one's goals.
- Willing to face any obstacle to achieve one's goals.

Intrinsic motivation or self-motivation is the best for children in the learning process. Yet every teacher at one time or the other is faced with the problem of motivating his students to learn. In such a situation, the teachers and parents may use certain methods of extrinsic or artificial motivation in order to motivate the children to learn.

How to motivate children to learn extrinsically ?

- encouraging self-confidence and positive attitude
- using child-centred approach
- setting definite purposes and goals
- using effective methods by teachers
- linking the new knowledge with the past experience and learning
- using rewards and praise
- acquainting them with the results and progress they have made
- using self-motivation graphs
- encouraging healthy competition (the learner competes, with his own past record)
- encouraging cooperation, team spirit and cooperative learning
- providing enough opportunities for independent learning and ego-involvement
- having appropriate learning situation and congenial atmosphere.

The secret of education lies in respecting the pupil.

— Ralph Waldo Emerson

In 2005, Sania Mirza's aim was to be among the top 50 in WTA, but her high motivation saw her reach the top 31 in the World Rankings of WTA

CHAPTER 7

MENTAL HYGIENE IN CHILDREN

Today, as compared to any other time in the past, we see that students are more prone to depression and suicide. So there is an urgent need to help maintain good mental health in children. The cooperation of the state authorities, parents, teachers, schools, colleges and other responsible members of the society is an urgent necessity to work for the good mental health of children. Uncongenial atmosphere at home, school and other situations bring harmful impact on the tender minds of children. Therefore, parents and others, who are responsible should be taken into confidence for achieving proper mental health of children.

WHAT IS MENTAL HYGIENE ?

Mental hygiene is that branch of hygiene which deals with the mental health of the individuals in the same way as physical hygiene is concerned with physical health and its aims, such as correct treatment and preventive measures. Mental hygiene is concerned with the preventions as well as treatment of mental illness, mental disorder and maintaining proper mental health, physical health and intellectual growth of the individual.

Lots of researches have taken place on mental hygiene. Let us see some of the definitions.

According to American Psychiatric Association, "Mental hygiene consists of measures to reduce the incidence of mental illness through prevention and early treatment and to promote mental health."

"Mental hygiene means investigation of the laws of mental health, and the taking or advocacy of measures for its preservation."

— Drever

"Mental hygiene is a science that deals with human welfare and pervades all fields of human relationships."

— Crow and Crow

From the definitions we can say that mental hygiene is a science which deals with preservation, promotion of mental health as well as prevention and treatment of mental disorders, diseases and other abnormalities.

MAIN CAUSES FOR POOR MENTAL HEALTH IN CHILDREN

(a) Hereditary Factors

(b) Constitutional Factors

(c) Environmental Factors

(a) Hereditary factors

In some cases of poor mental health and diseases, the causes are inherited from parents through defective genes. Certain inherited potentialities like the deficient intellectual ability also can cause poor mental health and nervous (system) diseases. Inappropriate physical structure and appearance cause some children to have inferiority complex and mental health problems. The hereditary factors are not under anyone's control. So the parents need to be prepared to accept these factors and make proper adjustments for the well being of their children.

(b) Constitutional or Physiological factors

As said above, certain physiological constitution and appearance can affect the mental health of the children. Poor physical health, physical defects, ailments and diseases are other factors which can affect the mental health of children. These factors can deteriorate one's strength and stamina for performing one's responsibilities. These can cause inferiority complexes and thus result in serious adjustment problems and poor mental health.

(c) Environmental factors

Man is the product of his environment. The famous environmentalist Watson, once said, "Give me any child and I will make him what you desire." This refers to the role of environment in the proper development of a child. If there is a rich and congenial environment, no child can become mentally maladjusted. The uncongenial environment at home, school, neighbourhood and society are responsible for social and emotional maladjustments in children. These maladjustments are the causes for mental illness in children.

Love and affection, acceptance, approval, appreciation and recognition are the cornerstones for good mental health in children. Lack of these make them feel rejected and emotionally insecure. The conflicts within the family, broken homes, lack of emotional and economic security cause anxities and other mental disorders in children. The behaviour and mental health of the parents and older members of the family, family atmosphere, the peer group and teacher relationships and the school environment have a direct bearing on the mental health of children.

AIMS OF MENTAL HYGIENE

There are mainly three important aims of mental hygiene. They are PREVENTIVE, PRESERVATIVE and CURATIVE - approaches.

PREVENTIVE AND PRESERVATIVE MEASURES :

The first and the best aim of mental hygiene would be to prevent oneself from the clutches of the negative environment and other factors which cause mental illness, maladjustment and mental disorder. Both preventive and preservative measures aim to make one aware of the following factors :

(a) To make aware of the factors which are responsible for poor mental health are the hereditary factors, the constitutional factors or physiological factors and environmental factors.

(b) To make aware of the various causes of maladjustment — personal as well as social.

(c) To make aware of the personal drives, needs, motives, conflicts, frustrations, tensions etc.

(d) To make aware of the ways and means of achieving emotional and social adjustment.

(e) To make individuals aware of their potentialities and inner resources.

(f) To make them aware that every individual is responsible for his own life and he has the right to make his own choice in life.

(g) To make individuals aware to accept and take responsibility for their circumstances and be courageous enough to take whatever initiative is necessary to creatively work their way through or around the challenges.

(h) To make individuals aware to develop a clear sense of their highest priorities and to live a focussed life with integrity.

(i) To make the individual aware that he is the creative force of his life.

(j) To make the individual aware that 'Creative Cooperation' and the master art of 'We' work better in life.

(k) To make the individuals identify and apply PRINCIPLES or NATURAL LAWS which govern a positive life have their source in God.

(l) To make the individuals aware that the greatest hygiene and fulfillment in life is serving others through self-actualization and self-transcendence.

(m) To make the individual aware to make use of all the opportunities to the fullest and achieve self-fulfillment.

(n) To help the individual to develop healthy human relationship and group interactions.

(o) To help the individual to develop good leadership which is plural – is a team effort.

The above points will go a long way to PREVENT and to PRESERVE (maintain) a GOOD MENTAL HEALTH.

CURATIVE MEASURES :

The priority of mental health should be to prevent and sustain good mental health. But in reality we come across that life is not all that easy and people fall victim to mental illness and disorders. So mental hygiene aims to treat the mental diseases and disorders.

(a) To give necessary knowledge regarding the types of mental illness, disorders and diseases.

(b) To suggest various forms of therapy for the treatment and curing of specific mental illness and disorders.

(c) To suggest the means for rehabilitation and readjustment of the maladjusted, mentally disturbed and mentally ill persons.

In this way, the ultimate aim of mental hygiene is, "to assist every individual in the attainment of fuller, happier, more harmonious and more effective existence."

— Shaffer and Shoben

WHAT CAN PARENTS, SCHOOL AND TEACHERS DO FOR THE GOOD MENTAL HEALTH OF CHILDREN ?

Both parents and teachers have the responsibility for the good mental health of children. First, the parents play the greatest role for the good mental health of children and the teachers have the responsibility to maintain it once the child starts school. The following vital points would be helpful for both parents and teachers:

1. Parents must meet the Psychological Needs of Children

The psychological needs like the physical needs must be met for the good mental health of children. These needs are; love and affection, acceptance and approval, appreciation and recognition. If these needs are met, children will spontaneously feel wanted, happy and emotionally secure. If they are not met they will feel rejected and emotionally insecure. No child she/he should feel that she/he is not wanted or accepted by his/her parents.

2. Good Children-Teacher Relationship

Teachers are the second parents. Children spend most of their day time with the teacher. So teachers also need to meet the psychological needs of children to some extent. The mental health of the students is very much influenced by the attitudes and behaviour of their teachers.

(a) *They need to be sympathetic and empathetic*
They should always have feelings of warmth and affection for their students.

(b) *Teachers need to be understanding*
Teachers need to understand and accept each student as a unique being.

A good teacher always understands the weak, average and above average students with dignity and care. She/he needs to be the supporter of the weak.

(c) *Teachers need to be proactice and show justice and equality*

Partiality, favouritism and partisan attitudes of the teacher always disturb students. Therefore, justice and equality shown by the teachers help in the proper mental health of children.

(d) Teachers need to be democratic in their dealings with the students.

(e) Teacher has to be a guide to the students in their pursuit of knowledge and personality development.

(f) *Consistent behaviour of the teacher*

Students get disturbed and confused if a teacher is inconsistent in her behaviour and attitude. When a student needs to be praised, praise him and when a correction is needed, correct him. This is important for the wholesome development of the student.

(g) *Having a positive attitude towards the students*

Positive attitude of teachers towards students works wonders. It helps the students to have a positive attitude towards themselves and towards each and every subject. Thus resulting in better adjustment and good mental health.

3. Good Physical Health

A sound body is said to possess a sound mind. Therefore, every care should be taken in maintaining good physical health in children. Both parents and teachers need to be alert and prompt in action to give appropriate medical care to children on time.

4. Proper Emotional Development

Students should be helped to maintain a balanced emotional state. They should be guided to exercise control over their emotions and to express them in a socially desirable manner.

5. Good Relationship with the Peers

Acceptance by peers is always desirable for good mental health in children. Nothing is more sad to the child than the rejection of himself by the group. Therefore, teachers need to take special care that each student is accepted by his classmates and others.

6. Go Slow on Perfection

Each student is unique and each one has her/his varying capacity. Each has his/her own way of working and studying. Therefore, the teacher should not push the children for perfect work. They should keep in mind that complete perfection is an ideal. Children should be accepted as they are, with their own strengths and weaknesses.

7. Encourage Healthy Competition and Discourage (Prevent) Unhealthy Competition

All are in the race of excelling and competing to achieve the best results. Students are always concerned about their grades and their place in the group. This leads to way for envy, jealousy, cheating, telling lies etc. Therefore, children should be encouraged to have a healthy competition. In a healthy competition, the student competes with his own previous record. While in an unhealthy competition, the student compares with others and he tries to compete with others. This kind of competition is harmful for students. So it should be absolutely discouraged.

8. Setting a Realistic Level of Aspiration

Students should be helped to know themselves, their interest, aptitudes, strengths and weaknesses, so that they can set a realistic goal which can be achieved through their sincere effort. The level of aspiration should neither be too high which they cannot achieve nor it should be very low which they can achieve with very little effort. In the present age, there are cases of students committing suicide due to this unrealistic level of aspiration which they set for themselves and sometimes by parents for them. So, for good mental hygiene in students, getting a realistic level of aspiration is very much desired.

9. Give Relevant and Appropriate Homework

Teachers need to assign homework with great care so that it is relevant and the amount of work is reasonable enough as well as the time required is available for children. Even during holidays, don't burden the children with homework.

10. Encourage Self-discipline

An atmosphere of reasonable freedom where a student can be spontaneous should prevail in the school and classroom. Teachers should encourage self-discipline in students on the democratic lines so that maintaining discipline becomes easier.

11. Encourage Children to have a Sense of Belongingness

Children need to feel that they belong to the school and the school belongs to them. This will help the students to share their responsibility to the school even after they leave school.

12. Give Opportunities for Outdoor Games

Most of the students have access to computers and they get glued to computer games. As a result, hardly anyone goes out for outdoor games or for a nature walk. Outdoor activities refresh and relaxes students. Therefore, both in school and at home they need to be engaged in outdoor activities.

13. Effective Methods of Teaching and Learning

Some best methods of teaching and learning are - learning by doing, from concrete to abstract, from known to unknown and co-operative learning. Children should be encouraged for creative thinking and discovery, and self-learning. Teachers need to be well-equipped to use various techniques of teaching. If not, children will lose interest in learning. Improper teaching methods bring a lot of dissatisfaction and tension in the minds of children. Lessons should always be planned according to the abilities and capacities of the students. While teaching, the teacher should keep in mind the individual difference of students. Encourage the use of head, heart and hand in learning.

14. Rich Curriculum with Extra Curricular Activities

A curriculum with only academic subjects will be disastrous for proper mental hygiene of children. There should be provision for extra curricular activities in the school timetable so that they would provide proper outlet for all the pent-up emotional energy. There should be other activities like painting / drawing / music / dance / sports /debates / quiz programmes so that they can express all their creative ideas. The above mentioned activities would bring positive results in children and proper mental health.

15. Sex Education

Our students are buying sex related information from the streets, from the media and from other sources which are quite misleading and harmful for them. Therefore, school should provide adequate sex education to the High School students.

16. Religious and Moral Values

When young boys and girls become adolescents, they are quite confused and frustrated to see the loss of moral and spiritual values which result in dishonesty, corruption, nepotism, injustice, inequality, unhealthy rivalry, lack of family values at home etc. Seeing these, they undergo mental conflicts, tensions and disorders. Therefore, schools must have adequate provision for religious and moral education.

17. Good Guidance Service

Every school should have guidance service to guide the students in their studies as well as for their personality development. Weaker students should be helped with diagnostic and remedial instructions. Under-achievers should be brought to their expected level and the 'gifted' should be given more challenging activities. So, all three catagories of students will be helped.

18. Good Mental Health of the Teachers

The good mental health of the students depends upon the mental health of the teachers. Teachers with sound mental health can improve the mental health of children. Good relationship with the authorities in the school has a great role for the sound mental health of the teachers.

Mutual understanding, give and take, and a positive attitude among colleagues also help the teachers to have a sound mental health. Teachers will have their own personal and professional problems but these can be solved if there is a good congenial atmosphere in the working place. Teachers need to be helped with understanding so that they can put their heart and soul in helping their students to have good mental health.

19. Help Children to accept themselves with their Strengths and Weaknesses

Students usually blame their own teachers, parents, situations, illness and their own fates when met with failures in examinations. They use defence mechanisms to protect themselves from any failure by blaming others or situations. Such type of protection is temporary. In the long run it can lead to serious mental conflicts and disorders. Therefore, children need to be helped to accept their weaknesses and strengths so that they will have the ability to face the failures in a healthy manner and work hard to improve their performance.

20. Child Guidance Clinic

Child guidance clinics by the state and other welfare organizations, and regular visits by psychiatrist and other mental experts to schools and colleges will also bring desirable results of good mental health in children.

Therefore, improving the mental health of children is a neccesity and it is a gigantic task of State Governments, parents, teachers and the school authorities.

CHAPTER 8

WHY DOES ONE FORGET?

"*I forgot the question's answer during the examination.' Oh! I forgot some important points of the essay I was writing." "My God! I forgot to put the question number in the answer paper."*

Mrs. Singh says, "I forgot to put salt in the curry." While Mrs. Kapur says that she kept the milk on the stove for boiling and went to take care of her mother-in-law in the next room who is sick and forgot about the milk.

All the above examples are common cases of forgetting in our everyday life which we are frequently acquainted with.

There are several known and unknown causes of forgetting. But before we go into the causes of forgetting, let us see what is forgetting ?

WHAT IS FORGETTING ?

When one fails to remember, recall or recognize something or someone from the past or when someone fails to do something, we say, he or she has forgotten to do it. We have thousands of experiences and kinds of things to remember in our life. To remember all these without forgetting will be a difficult task. Therefore, forgetting is a natural thing to happen in life. In some cases, forgetting is good in our life, otherwise life would have been miserable. But at the same time excessive and unusual forgetting is harmful to us.

Let us see some definitions given by eminent personalities on forgetting.

"Forgetting means failure at any time to recall an experience, when attempting to do so, or to perform an action previously learned."

— Drever

"Forgetting is the loss, permanent or temporary, of the ability to recall or recognize something learned earlier."

— Munn

According to the above definitions, forgetting is termed as a failure or a loss, either permanent or temporary to recall, recognize and reproduce. Forgetting is just the opposite of remembering and essentially a failure in the ability of reproducing.

KINDS OF FORGETTING

From life experiences we can say that there are two kinds of forgetting.

1. Passive or Natural Forgetting

2. Active or Morbid Forgetting

1. Passive or Natural Forgetting

"I forgot the person's name who was sitting next to me during the long flight from New York to Bombay though we shared quite a bit of ourselves."

This is passive forgetting. The kind of forgetting in which there is no intention of forgetting on the part of the individual is known as passive or natural forgetting. In this kind of forgetting, one does not have to make any deliberate effort to forget. In a quite normal way, with the lapse of time, one gradually forgets so many things experienced and learned earlier.

2. Active or Morbid Forgetting

It is also known as abnormal forgetting. "I don't want to remember the sad experience I had with one of my colleagues."

In this forgetting, one deliberately tries to forget something. This kind of forgetfulness, as Freud explains, originates from repression. Under this process, the painful experience and bitter memories are deliberately pushed into the unconscious layer of the mind and are left there for forgetting.

WHY DO WE FORGET ?

In some cases, it is simple to understand why one forgets - while in most cases of forgetting, it is a difficult task to answer, why does one forget ?

THE CAUSES OF FORGETTING :

1. Lack of Interest

If we have no interest to know a person we will forget that person even if we have spent few years working with him. In the same way, if the child had no interest and motivation to learn something, certainly his retention would be very poor and he would not be able to recall or reproduce the matter he had tried to learn.

2. Forces of Distraction

If students are distracted while learning they will never be able to recall the whole matter. If the environment is full of distractions, the child will not be able to concentrate and learn.

3. Inadequate Impression at the Time of Learning

If the learning material is not impressive while learning, it will be difficult to recall. Inadequate or improper learning is likely to be forgotten. Sometimes, we do not care for certain matter or topic because they don't impress us. It results in no impression. This type of inadequate impression at the time of learning, in most cases, can be discovered as a real cause of forgetting.

4. Lack of Intention and Will to Learn

Whatever is learnt with good intention and will, will be remembered better. For example, a child works hard in order to beat his previous record in the exam will surely bring in a better result.

5. Day Dreaming among the Older Students

Day dreaming while learning or while listening in the class results in poor retention and thereby poor recall and reproduction.

6. Lapse of Time

What is learnt or experienced is forgotten with the lapse of time. Psychologists have tried to name this cause as the passive decay through disuse. With the passage of time through disuse, the memory traces or the impression of what we learnt gets weaker and weaker, and finally fades away.

7. Active Forgetting

Certain things are forgotten by people purposely. In some cases, people avoid remembering certain events or situations. Recalling such events in later life will be difficult. Similarly, some people tend to forget the painful experiences or names of the people they don't like. This is also called repression.

8. Lack of Review

Students tend to forget the learned matter if it is not revised from time to time.

9. Poor Habit of Learning

10. Lack of Planning and Organization in Learning

11. Fatigue

Learning and recalling are impossible when one is tired physically and mentally.

12. Anxiety and Rise of Emotions

A student forgets to take her hall ticket for the examination and becomes anxious. As a result she forgets some answers during the exam.

A teacher trainee forgot to take her lesson plans which she had to hand over to her supervising lecturer before she starts her lesson in the class. This made her very upset and she even forgot to use her teaching aids and as a whole, she made a mess of her teaching lesson.

The above two cases are of anxiety producing examples which cause forgetting. In other words, anxiety causes forgetfulness and forgetfulness causes anxiety. In the same way, when one is taken over by emotions like fear, anger or love, one forgets what one had learned or experienced before hand. Students' exam phobia is a very good example of anxiety and rise of emotions. Musicians, orators and actors fail miserably on the stage when they become panicky and forget their prepared music, speech or dialogue.

A student whose mother is sick will have some fear and anxiety during the exam and it will affect his/her performance in the examination.

13. Poor Health and Disturbed Mental State

When a student is sick he fails to concentrate while learning. His retention becomes poor and his recall and recognition will be affected too. When one is mentally disturbed his recalling of learned matter will be very difficult. Brain injury may also cause forgetting.

14. Lower IQ or Mental Defects

Individuals with lower IQ or suffering from mental defects have been generally found to be very poor in retention and recall.

15. Alternation of Stimulus Condition

Children forget when they have alternation of the stimulus conditions between the time of learning and the time of recall. For example, a child who learnt the meaning of butterfly and birds with the help of pictures, feels confused in naming them in the absence of such pictures.

16. Interference of Association

In the words of Morgan "we forget because in large part, associations interferes with one another."

This means we forget something because what we have learned previously, interferes with the remembering of what we learn afterwards.

The interfering effects of association can work both ways, both forward and backward. The psychological terms used for these types of interference are 'Proactive Inhibition' and 'Retroactive Inhibition.'

Proactive Inhibition

Here, what one has learned previously, (say matter, A) interferes with the memory of what one learns afterwards (matter, B) = A – B.

In other words, when one tries to remember or recall the present learnt matter (B), the previously learnt matter (A) comes and interferes with it.

Retroactive Inhibition

Retroactive inhibition is just the reverse of proactive inhibition. Here, the later learning activity or matter (B) somehow works backward to interferes or inhibits the matter of earlier learning (A) = B – A.

In both the cases, it can be easily seen that similar experiences, when they follow each other, produce more interferences than dissimilar experiences.

In addition to the above mentioned factors there are so many other factors which are responsible for forgetting. They can be named as chronic and long illness, lack of purpose, unfavourable situations or conditions at the time of learning and reproduction.

GUIDANCE TO CHILDREN

It is clear that the above factors are responsible for forgetfulness. Therefore, every care should be taken to remove these obstacles and ensure a congenial atmosphere and environment for effective learning. Young children should be guided for a healthy habit of learning. Don't make them force to learn if they are not ready. Also don't make them sit and learn for a long time because they have a very short span of attention. Since they are not ready for abstract thinking, they should be provided with concrete learning materials and objects. Proper associations and relationships must also be established so that learned matter may be retained for a longer time and can be recalled rapidly.

Try to provide a healthy environment for the child so that he can concentrate on the learning without any fear, anger or anxiety. The child should be provided with enough outdoor and indoor exercises so that he gets enough opportunities for necessary outlet and catharsis of his pent-up energy and emotions. A democratic environment full of affection, security and love should prevail at home and in the school, and it should be seen that no child develops any sort of complex in his mind. The child should also be trained for good learning habits so that he can be saved from the wastage resulting from forgetting.

CHAPTER 9

TRAINING IN MEMORY

WHAT IS MEMORY ?

In our day-to-day life we have a very complex network of learning experiences. These learning experiences are retained properly in the form of mental impressions or images so that they can be revived when we need them. In the psychological world this ability of retention and repeating is known as 'Memory'.

Let us examine some of the definitions given by psychologists.

"Memory consists in remembering what has previously been learned."

— Woodworth and Marquis

"The power that we have to 'store' our experiences, and to bring them into the field of consciousness sometime after the experiences have occured, is termed memory."

— Ryburn

As these definitions state, our memory is regarded as a special ability of our mind to conserve or store what has been previously learned or experienced in the form of memory images or traces (engrams) to recall or reproduce them after sometime. It is a complex process which involves all the four factors of memory; learning, retention, recall and recognition.

FACTORS OF MEMORY

(a) Learning

In the process of remembering or memorization, learning or experiencing something is the primary condition on the first stage.

For example, a child learnt the name of a bird - parrot, and about it.

(b) Retention

Retention is the second stage. At this stage the learning experiences are retained in the form of mental images or traces. This preservation of the memory traces by our central nervous system or brain is known as retaining of the learned matter or experienced act. How long one can retain depends upon the strength and quality of the memory traces. If we go back to the example of the bird – parrot, which the child learnt, we'll see that the child has retained the name parrot, the colour of the feather, the shape of the beak and the colour of the beak of the parrot etc.

(c) Recognition

This is recognizing or becoming aware of an object, person or situation as presented to him earlier. Recognition is easier and simple because the presence of the object is there and he has to only recognize it. For example, the bird parrot is presented to the child and he recognizes it as a parrot according to his previous learning experience.

(d) Recall

The fourth stage recalling is what has been learned earlier. For example, if the child is able to remember all about the parrot which the teacher had told him, its food habits etc., then we can say he was able to recall about the bird, parrot. If the memory traces are strong, then the retention is good and the recall of the past experiences will be easily possible.

A good memory is able to recognize, recall and reproduce the relevant ideas, things or persons at the proper time.

TYPES OF MEMORY

Individuals are found to differ in the power of memorization. Consequently, they are said to possess one or the other type of memory. The nature of the tasks which are imposed upon our memory at different times and under different circumstances demand each time a particular type of memory. Therefore, we make use of one or the other type of memory according to our need. Some of the important types of memory with relevance to their nature are given below:

1. Immediate Memory

Immediate memory is needed when we want to remember a thing for a short period of time and then forget it. For example, our seat/berth no. in a train or the seat no. in a plane. After our use or journey we forget it.

2. Permanent Memory

Whatever we remember permanently is permanent memory. Remembering our names, our parents' names, date of birth etc., are examples of permanent memory.

3. Rote Memory

When things are learnt without understanding their meaning, it is called rote memory. For example, children learning the nursery rhymes.

4. Logical Memory

It is based on logical thinking and reasoning. It takes into consideration the purposeful and insightful learning. The learner tries to understand what he learns and why he learns.

5. Associative Memory

Individuals associate the present learning with the previously learned things and with many related things and establish multiple connections. This is called associative memory. It refers that the learning or memorization of a particular thing is not done in isolation. One tries to connect or associate it with as many other things as one can. It will help one's memory to maintain multiple relationships.

6. Active Memory

In active memory, one tries to remain active or make deliberate attempts for recalling or recognizing past experiences. For example, a student during his exam makes use of this type of memory.

7. Passive Memory

In passive memory, the past experiences are recalled spontaneously without any serious attempt or will. For example, a particular food item at the table will easily remind one about her/his mother and all the various food items she used to prepare at home.

METHODS OF MEMORIZATION
OR
REMEMBERING

The problem of having lack of time and lots of matter for memorizing something has persuaded many psychologists to devise various methods of memorization. The following are some of the methods :

1. Recitation Method

In this method the learner first reads the matter once or twice and then tries to recall and recite that without looking at the material. For example, students learn poems, speeches etc.

2. Whole and Part Methods

It involves two methods. First, for example, learning a poem; the individual reads the whole poem again and again from the beginning till the end. This is called whole method of memorization. The second method is learning the poem part by part by dividing it and memorizing it separately. This is called part method.

Both of these methods have advantages as well as disadvantages. It depends on the nature and length of the matter. The whole method is found better than the part method in case of memorizing a short poem or a speech which requires less time, while part method proves better if the poem is a longer one. In some cases, a combination of these two methods has been found suitable.

3. Spaced and Unspaced Methods

In the spaced method of memorization, the child is not required to memorize the assigned material in one continuous sitting. After memorizing for sometime, some rest is provided and in this way the principle of 'Work and rest' is followed in this method.

In unspaced method of memorization, the child has to memorize the assigned material at one sitting without any interval or rest. Hence, in this method, the memorization is done continuously without interruption till it is mastered.

IMPROVING THE MEMORY OF CHILDREN

HOW CAN WE IMPROVE THE MEMORY OF CHILDREN ?

Each and every parent will be happy to know how we can improve the memory of children. Whether memory can be improved by training or not, is a controversial issue. But its improvement or training is a commonly expressed desire on the part of every individual. Some experts say that memory training is not possible and it is not like muscle training.

"Memory training is not like muscle training. You can make a muscle develop by any kind of use. Memory is not helped by any kind of exercise."

— Dr. Morgan and Gilliland

But we cannot lose hope of having a good memory and how we can improve and sustain a good memory. There is some possibility of improving the memory because as discussed earlier, memory consists of four factors - learning, retention, recognition and recall. Improvement in any one or more of the constituents is likely to improve the memory as a whole. Therefore, the question regarding the improvement of memory, for its logical answer can be broken into four different areas.

They are :
- Is improvement in learning possible ?
- Is improvement in retention possible ?
- Is improvement in recall possible ?
- Is improvement in recognition possible ?

Improvement in retention by training is not possible since it is native and inherited. At the most, one can try to protect the retentiveness by some hygienic measures and by the law of use from time to time. But it is hardly possible to improve it by training. It is difficult to improve recognition also by training since it happens very promptly and spontaneously.

The other two factors, learning and recall, have been observed to be improved by training. Since learning is the primary factor let us see how learning can be improved.

"A good memory depends on good and effective learning." Therefore, if the learning is improved, the memory also can be improved. All our best attempts in the field of education are directed to make the pupil learn properly. An effective learning leaves behind strong memory images or traces which are conserved in the form of 'engrams' in the brain. Strong memory images give better retention. Therefore, improvement of memory to a large extent depends upon this factor which can be improved by training. Learning can be improved by improving the following factors :

I. THE FACTORS WITHIN THE LEARNER :

(a) The physical and mental state of the learner

A good healthy physical state of the learner helps in effective learning and retention. The balanced mental state of the individual is also essential for good learning without any interruption and distraction. For example, a child who is sick cannot concentrate properly while learning. A pleasant, happy mind helps in learning.

(b) Will to learn

There must be a firm determination or a strong will to learn for achieving desired success in learning. 'Where there is a will there is a way'. The stronger the will to learn, the better the registration of the matter in the brain as memory images. Matter read, heard or seen without intention is difficult to be remembered at later times.

(c) Purpose and aim

A learner who learns with a purpose and aim will never give up learning and he'll use all his might to learn well and remember well. As a result, recall and reproduction of the learned matter becomes easier.

(d) Interest and attention

Interest and close attention are essential for effective learning and memorization. One who has no interest in what one learns, cannot give due attention to it and consequently will not be able to learn it. The words of Mr. Bhatia gives the importance of interest and attention for memory in the following words:

"Interest is the mother of attention and attention is the mother of memory; if you would secure memory, you must first catch the mother and the grandmother."

II. THE EXTERNAL FACTORS :

(a) Adopting proper methods of memorization

There are several methods of memorization but all are not suitable on all occasions and for all individuals. Therefore, a judicious selection should be made in choosing a particular method in a given situation.

(b) Follow the principle of association

Nothing should be learnt in isolation. Attempts should be made to connect it with one's previous learning on the one hand and with many related things on the otherhand. Sometimes, for association of ideas special techniques and devices are used that facilitate learning and recall.

(c) Grouping and rhythm

Grouping and rhythm also facilitate learning and help in remembering. For example, a telephone no. 612222668 can be easily grouped and memorized and recalled as 612, 222, 668. There are various common rhythms arranged for easy recall, e.g., the days of each month. Thirty days are Sept... etc....

(d) Utilizing as many senses as possible

Help children to use as many senses as possible while learning. Not only the eyes and hands, but the senses of touch and feel, smell, taste etc. Therefore, audio-visuals and other concrete objects give better impression at the time of learning. Better impression results in good memory.

(e) Arranging better learning conditions

Environmental factors also affect the learning process. A calm and quiet atmosphere is suitable for better learning. A stimulating environment at home and at school are equally important for better learning.

(f) Parental attitude

Motivating and encouraging parents at all times are a great strength for children to learn better.

(g) Effective methods and techniques

Use effective methods and techniques that will facilitate children to use the three domains of learning, which will in turn help the children to learn better and ensure better retention and permanent memory. The three domains of learning are – cognitive, affective and psychomotor or conative. These will include knowing (cognitive), positive feeling (affective) and applying it in life or using it in daily life (conative). In other words, it is learning by head, heart and hand. If these techniques are followed in learning, no child will forget the learning experience he had. 'Learning by doing' uses all these domains of a person.

(h) Provide change and proper rest

Adequate rest, sleep and change of work should be made for children, they help to reduce fatigue and monotony. Children need a minimum of eight hours sleep for a healthy mind and body. A fresh mind is necessary to learn better and to retain it for a longer time.

(i) Follow the law of exercise and law of use

Children need lots of varieties of exercises and drill to learn joyfully and enthusiastically. Varieties of excercises and drills will remove all the burden and dullness from children. An intelligent repetition with full understanding always helps in effective learning and permanent retention.

Using the learning experiences and applying them in their life will help in recalling and lasting memory. Lack of use of what is learned causes the memory traces to get weaker and weaker and finally be forgotten. Therefore, a lot of care should be taken for drill, repetition practice, review and usage of the matter from time to time for good memory.

(j) Revision without delay

Whatever one has learned has to be reviewed as early as possible. This always helps in recalling any learned matter for recalling later. For example, whatever a student studied in the school on Monday and revised it on the same evening (Monday) before going to bed, the child will be able to recall better, to use it for a class test on Wednesday. Thus prompt revision helps in the improvement of recall.

(k) Be free from excessive anxiety, fear and other emotional factors which may block memory while recalling.

(l) Be positive and have confidence

One should never think that he/she would not be able to recall something. Have confidence in oneself. Be calm and quiet and avoid nervousness. One should be sure that she/he is able to recall everything.

(m) Make association while recalling

Making associations while learning and recalling help in memory. For example, Children's day is Pandit Nehru's Birthday. Give a break when one finds it difficult to remember something. Don't fight oneself to recall something. The more one fights, the more one will find it difficult to recall. When one finds it difficult to recall, give a break for the time-being and later one may be surprised to see that whatever he/she wanted to recall may be coming in his mind without any effort.

The factors we've discussed above may be of great help in training to improve the memory of children. There may be some other creative ways which certain individuals apply on their own for better recall and reproduction.

On completion of her graduation

Holding her OSCAR award for the documentary
— Hellen Keller In Her Story (1954)

HELEN KELLER
(June 27, 1880 – June 1, 1968)

Helen Keller was an American author, political activist and lecturer.

A deaf-blind woman who became an inspiration, and an example of courage to all mankind.

At the age of 24, in 1904, she completed her graduation, becoming the first deaf-blind person to earn a Bachelor of Arts degree.

She devoted her life to illuminate the darkness by giving voice to disabled persons, especially blind and handicapped.

Although a handicapped child, but she lived as 'The Gifted' one.

CHAPTER 10

EXCEPTIONAL CHILDREN

Wilma Rudolph *was born a tiny premature baby. She caught pneumonia, then scarlet fever and finally polio. The polio left one leg badly crippled, with her foot twisted inward. Until the age of eleven, Wilma hobbled around on metal braces. Then she asked her sister to keep watch while she practised walking without the braces. She kept this up everyday, afraid that her parents might discover what she was doing and she might be compelled to stop. Eventually, feeling guilty, she told her doctor, who was flabbergasted. However, he gave her permission to continue, but only for a short period of time.*

Wilma worked away at it until she eventually threw away her crutches for good. She progressed to running, and by the time she was sixteen she won a bronze medal in a relay race in Melbourne Olympics. Four years later, in the Rome olympics, she became the first woman in history to win three gold medals in track and field.

She returned to a ticker-tape welcome in the U.S.A., had a private meeting with President Kennedy, and received the Sullivan award as the nation's top amateur athelete.

WHO ARE EXCEPTIONAL CHILDREN ?

Exceptional children are those who show a significant deviation from what is supposed to be the normal or average to their group. These children are exceptionally inferior or superior to the normal children in terms of physical development, mental ability, social behaviour and emotional behaviour. Their special needs and education have to be met for their proper adjustment and maximum utilization of their abilities. If not, they will experience maladjustments in their life.

Crow and Crow have given the following definition for the term exceptional :

"The term 'atypical' or 'exceptional' is applied to a trait or to a person possessing the trait if the extent of deviation from normal possession of the trait is so great that because of it the individual warrants or receives special attention from his fellows and his behaviour responses and activities are thereby affected."

CLASSIFICATION OF EXCEPTIONAL CHILDREN

Thus, the term "exceptional children" covers a wide range. These exceptional children can be grouped into several categories according to their exception.

The following are the different classifications of exceptional children :

(*i*) The Backward Children or the Slow Learners

(*ii*) The Physically Handicapped

(*iii*) The Mentally Retarded

(*iv*) (*a*) The Socially Handicapped or Delinquents and

     (*b*) Emotionally Maladjusted

(*v*) The Gifted Children

I. THE BACKWARD OR SLOW LEARNERS

Slow learners being helped individually

WHO ARE BACKWARD CHILDREN OR SLOW LEARNERS ?

Backward children are slow learners and they find it difficult to keep pace with the normal work. Let us examine a few definitions.

"Backwardness in general is applied to cases where their educational attainment falls below the level of their natural abilities."

— Barton Hall

"A backward child is one who when compared with other pupils for the same chronological age showed marked educational deficiencies."

— Schonell

"A backward child is one who in mid-school career is unable to do the work of the class below that which is normal for his age."

— Burt

The above definitions give us the various characteristics of backward children.

(a) Backward children are slow learners and their educational attainment falls below the level of their natural abilities.

(b) They find it difficult to keep pace with the normal work.

(c) These children fall behind children of their age academically and usually remain in the same class for a number of years.

(d) They find it difficult to learn with the children in lower classes and who are younger to them in age.

(e) Like mentally retarded children, we cannot call a child backward merely on the basis of his IQ. In fact, on one hand, intelligence is no guarantee against backwardness. On the other hand, a lower IQ does not make a child backward. Consequently, the backward child should not be labelled mentally retarded or dull. **Barton Hall has emphasized this fact in the following words :**

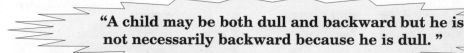

"A child may be both dull and backward but he is not necessarily backward because he is dull. "

KINDS OF BACKWARDNESS

(a) General Backwardness

General backwardness is where the child is found to be weak in all the subjects of the school curriculum.

(b) Specific Backwardness

Specific backwardness is where the child lags behind or is weak in one or two specific subjects while in others he shows satisfactory or even extraordinary progress.

Causes of Backwardness

The causes of backwardness is an individual's problem and every individual's problem is unique. It is certain that the roots of backwardness is within him/her or outside in the environment. It is also found that there are so many causes that operate together in a particular type of backwardness.

The following are some causes of backwardness :

(A) FACTORS WITHIN THE CHILD

1. The Physiological or Physical Factors

The physiological and physical conditions of the child at every stage affects his educational attainments. Studies of Burt, Schonell and others have shown that the majority of the educationally backward children suffer from some kind of development or physical retardation. They are either born with poor health and physical deformities or become the victims of poor environment and thus suffer from physical ailments, chronic diseases such as heart, kidney and bodily defects. The bodily defects like defective vision, faulty hearing, speech defects etc., handicap these children. Children who fall ill due to some serious illness lose attendance in school and thus fall back. These children may develop into educational backwardness because they find it difficult to cope up with the rest of the class.

2. Intellectual Factors

Some children are born with brain defects or intellectual sub-normality. These intellectually inferior children cannot keep pace and prove to be slow learners. Burt, on the basis of his studies asserts that, "In the majority of cases, defective intelligence or lower IQ has been found to be the sole cause of backwardness." We also find that students whose intellectual powers like thinking and reasoning, concentration, observation and imagination are not properly developed generally drift towards backwardness. These children also suffer from emotional imbalance and social maladjustment which impedes progress in school subjects.

3. The Environmental Factors

(a) Home Influences

(i) The privileged homes and well-to-do families are able to provide amenities of living and proper facilities for educating the children, but in poor families not only the educational facilities but also the most essential necessities of life are denied to the children. Due to unhygienic conditions and malnutrition, the health of these children is affected. It reduces their learning capacity and thus makes them backward. These children also do not get opportunities for gaining richer experiences in the form of internet, social contacts, excursions, reading material etc. Consequently the child finds it difficult to grasp the ideas related to these experiences. Also in poor homes, the children are required to perform many household chores or to help in family occupation. As a result they devote less time to their studies and are also too tired to pay proper attention at home as well as in school.

(ii) The intellectual inferiority and illiteracy of parents also contribute towards sub-normal educational attainments. Such parents neither possess a positive attitude towards education nor do they have the ability to guide and help them in their studies. Lack of motivation from parents affect these children.

(iii) The family relationship and behaviour of the family members also contribute much in this direction. Strained relationships and improper behaviour creates many emotional and social problems. Homes where there is divorce between parents or where the parental attitudes are too hard or indulgent, the child's psychological and social needs are not satisfied. In such an environment, the child neither feels secure nor gets proper love, affection and guidance from his parents and hence becomes educationally backward.

(b) School Influences

Improper school atmosphere and unfavourable conditions also contribute to the problem of backwardness. The following factors operative in school affect the educational attainment of children:

(i) Defective methods, uninteresting and ineffective teaching.

(ii) Lack of equipment, facilities and provision for revision, experimental and creative work, co-curricular activities and varied experiences etc.

(iii) Defective curriculum and examination system.

(iv) Lack of guidance and wrong choices made in the selection of subjects by children.

(v) Poor administration and indiscipline.

(vi) Lack of proper motivation.

(vii) Improper attitude of the teacher and inter-personal relationships among the staff-members and students.

(c) Neighbourhood and Social Agencies

The social environment of the child is not confined to the home or school. The neighbourhood where the child lives, the group with whom he plays and associates with, the press, radio, cinema, clubs etc., all contribute to the problem of educational sub-normality. It may colour his attitude towards life, work or studies and also divert his attention to other socially undesirable activities in place of school studies and consequently causes backwardness.

Needs of backward children

Just like any other child, the backward child also has the need for love, acceptance, recognition, belongingness etc. But he has few special needs like need for special and individual care and attention, individual help to come out of his backwardness and improve himself, and need for better facilities etc.

GUIDANCE, EDUCATION AND REMEDY FOR BACKWARD CHILDREN

The first task in planning for the guidance, education and remedy of the backward child is to ascertain the possible and more probable causes of backwardness. Therefore, diagnosis of the causes is priority.

Diagnosis of the Causes

Diagnosis can be done in the following ways :

1. Attainment tests and diagnostic tests should be used to assess the extent and nature of backwardness in specific subjects.

2. Use intelligence tests to know the IQ.

3. The special abilities of the child should be ascertained by means of psychological tests.

4. The child's behaviour as a whole and his specific behaviour in particular situations should be observed. His emotional characteristics, social relationships and temperament should be assessed.

5. A thorough physical and medical examination is also essential for knowing the condition of the child. A history of the child's development from infancy with regard to physical ailments and disabilities, and defects should be studied.

6. The socio-economic status of the child's family, the living conditions, education of the parents, size of the family, birth orders, relationship with the family, the nature of the group and the social environment in which the child is living should also be carefully studied.

7. The school environment, including methods of teaching, facilities available for co-curricular activities, student-teacher interaction should be carefully assessed.

8. The academic history of the child should be properly studied.

EDUCATIONAL GUIDANCE AND REMEDY FOR CHILDREN

The remedy for backwardness not only lies solely in its nature and extent but as well as the causes which produce it. There is no single or simple remedy applicable to every case of backwardness. Each case is unique and therefore needs individual attention and planned treatment. The following points may prove helpful in planning an educational programme :

1. Regular medical check-up and necessary treatment

In case of backwardness, where physical defects and ill-health are found to be contributing factors, there is a need for regular medical check-up. So school authorities, with the co-operation of the parents, should take steps for the treatment of such children.

2. Re-adjustment in the home and school

Backward children have temperamental and emotional difficulties and suffer from mental conflicts. Such mentally perturbed children need love, affection and security. There should be a close contact with the parents so that the root causes of emotional and mental disturbances are discovered. Parents also need education for the proper handling of these students. The social agencies and government should come forward not only for educating the parents but also for giving proper attention to remove the handicaps caused to children due to poverty and other social maladies.

3. Provision for special schools and classes

Under this provision, backward children are segregated from other children and kept in small groups either in special classes or in special schools. Emphasising the need for such segregation, professor Udai Shankar says : "If they are kept with normals, they will be pushed back and the backward will become more backward with children of their own level, but they will be less conscious of their drawbacks and they will feel more secure in the group of their own type where there will be more encouragement and appreciation and less competition."

But complete segregation in the form of separate schools is often criticized and it does not provide opportunities for mingling freely with normal children and thus derive rich experiences in their company. Therefore, a via-media should be adopted. These backward children as far as possible should be taught in the same schools but special care and attention may be paid to them. Thus, instead of separate schools, keep them in the normal school with other children but with special care and attention.

4. Provision of special curriculum, methods of teaching and special teachers should be provided

The group of children suffering with acute backwardness rightly deserves special care meant for normal children. It should include more practical and concrete aspects so that they may be made competent workers and intelligent citizens rather than scholars. Methods of teaching should be modified. They require short and simple methods based on concrete living experiences. Concrete materials, appropriate aids and rich direct experiences should be provided to such children. Also, they should be taught by special trained teachers.

5. Special coaching and proper individual attention

When the area and nature of weakness is spotted through proper tests in various subjects, arrangement for special coaching should be made for backward children individually and collectively as the situation demands. It can be given in terms of more practice, drill, repetition, review or explanation.

6. Checking truancy and non-attendance

Backwardness in some cases is due to irregular attendance. The causes for truancy should be discovered and steps should be taken to remove them.

7. Provision of co-curricular activities and rich experience

In some cases, backwardness is caused due to lack of interest in the school studies. The child does not find anything challenging or stimulating in the routine class, therefore provision should be made for varied methods and rich experiences in the form of co-curricular activities and instructional programmes.

8. Maintenance of a proper progress record

Cumulative record, the child profile card, anecdote card, psychological tests given, should be regularly and accurately maintained.

9. Rendering guidance services

In every school guidance services should be organized well. The authorities should pay attention in making parents conscious of their child's ability, interests and aptitudes, and accordingly aspire for careers for their children.

10. Controlling negative environmental factors

The social surroundings or peer group influences play a dominant role in colouring one's interests, attitudes, ambitions and visions of life. Therefore, due care should be taken to remove or at least reduce the influence of these negative enviornmental factors which are responsible for the backwardness of children.

11. Take the help of experienced educational psychologist

Educational psychologists may give valuable guidance to the teachers as well as parents for taking remedial steps in removing the causes of backwardness in their children.

The problem of these children are multidimensional and complicated. Therefore, not only the teachers or school authorities but parents, educational psychologists, social workers and state authorities should join their hands together in discovering and rectifying the causes of backwardness in children.

II. THE PHYSICALLY HANDICAPPED

 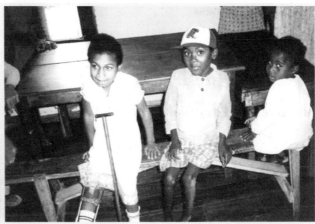

The children those who suffer from chronic illness or crippling defects to the extent that their educational progress, social functioning and vocational or job opportunities are adversely affected compared with their physically able-mates, they are considered as physically handicapped children. For example, a polio affected child is held back from a running race where his able-mates are participating in it.

The physically handicapped can be subdivided into a wide range of disabilities :

1. Those who suffer from **sensory handicap** like sight (blind, partially blind), hearing (deaf, hard of hearing) and speech.

2. The **orthopaedically handicapped**, the crippled who have difficulty in movement.

3. Those who suffer from **organic disorders** having diseases like epilepsy or encephalitis or those who have endocrinological imbalance causing behavioural problems.

4. Those who have **specific disabilities** like dyslexia, disgraphia, apraxia, word blindness and word deafness.

5. In addition, the chronically ill who may have health problems such as T.B., heart defects, allergies, diabetes, rheumatism etc., also fall in the category of the handicapped.

Some of the physically handicapped are born with one or more of these disabilities, others acquire them after birth as a result of accidents, infections, organic defects or glandular malfunctioning. The disability in each condition varies from very slight, where the child is not too different from normal children, to total dependence on others for the maintenance of life itself.

1. SENSORY DEFECTS

(A) VISUAL :

The five senses are the gateways of learning. Of these, sight is the master sense that opens up all channels of knowledge to the infant.

Causes of Blindness

Some causes of blindness are accidents, injuries, trachoma, glaucoma, cataracts, small-pox, squint, short-sightedness, malnutrition and paucity of medical services. These are preventable and curable. While some are born blind and the adjustments they have to make are much more difficult.

Guidance and Education for the Blind

The blind or the partially sighted can take care of themselves to an extent and can be productive.

Today many are being absorbed in open industries and in typical jobs which they are able to do. The Central Government has provided certain number of quota to these category of people. What is important is that proper education and training need to be given according to their abilities and the interests so that they can be of service to themselves and others.

These children need to be guided in their education, training and adjustment. There are specialists who provide the right type of educational facilities, apparatus and appliances to educate them. The knowledge of braille reading and manual skills which need to be acquired by the blind to a certain precision is the work of special institutions which cater to the blind. The blind individual has to be guided to make adjustments in life through other social and co-curricular activities. He can be helped to learn certain basic skills of reading, writing, climbing and moving independently. Once he has acquired these skills, he can be treated like any other normal individual and may even be put in a regular school with the normal children.

Feelings of insecurity, inferiority and dependence make them completely depressed and heartbroken. Parents of such children can be overprotective and may make them very dependent on them. Parents of such children need a lot of guidance in rearing them and in the environmental opportunities they need to provide. Society and teachers need to be guided in the development to strengthen the right attitudes to them and not treat them with pity but provide them with opportunities to maximise their inner growth and development.

The National Association for the Blind, New Delhi (India) has coordinated the efforts of all the private and the social institutions. Not only a number of blind schools have been opened but also industrial homes, workshops for the blind and sheltered workshops for the benefit of training and employment. Most of the cities in India have these facilities.

(B) DEAFNESS :

Deafness can be classified into three definite degrees.
  (i)   Born deaf, resulting in no language formation and no speech development and therefore called deaf and mute.
 (ii)   Having partial impairment of hearing capacity, resulting in delayed development and also adjusting to hearing aids.
(iii)   Deafness in later years due to injury etc.

Causes of Deafness

Congenital deafness may occur due to prenatal infection such as influenza, typhoid, high fever in the mother, causing injury to the germplasm. Deafness may be acquired later in life due to infection of throat or conditions like high fever, meningitis and encephalitis.

Diagnosing the Defect and Damage Correctly

Before providing educational facilities to the deaf, the damage and defect have to be detected accurately. Once this is achieved, the children can be classified according to their hearing capacity and group instruction would be possible.

Guidance and Education for the Deaf

Whatever degree of deafness an individual suffers from, his means of communication is disturbed and this will cause a tremendous setback in his social and economic life. They will find adjustment very difficult. They will be found depressed and introverted. So they need empathetic understanding from family and friends.

For the profoundly deaf, education has to be provided in special schools where expert guidance can be given by trained technical personnel. The partially deaf or those having impaired hearing may after high reading and auditory training be adjusted to regular schools. Care should be taken to see that teachers and classmates understand the basic acoustic problems of such a child and not make him a victim of ridicule or fun.

(C) SPEECH :

Speech disorders are commonly referred to as 'stammering' and 'stuttering'.

In stammering, the individual makes a number of halts or pauses and hesitates when speaking. Stuttering is regarded as a more violent form of stammering in which the halts breaks and repetitions are many more. The speech disorders are very obviously noticed and the child feels extremely ashamed to talk in strange situations or with strangers. In some cases, it is found that a child stammers only in certain situations like, public speaking or when faces a new place or stress. In some cases, the child stutters only at home or in school while in some cases the child may stutter only infront of an authority figure.

Causes of Stammering

It is more psychological than physical and rarely hereditary. It is usually noticed at the age of three to four years. In some cases when young boys turn teenagers, they develop stammering. This is due to their sudden change in voice, they become self-conscious or they are rediculed by others. This is a psychological problem and this can be corrected.

If physical, it is caused by neuromuscular incoordination of the group of muscles concerned with respiratioin and articulation. If psychological, it is due to a number of uncongenial factors prevalent in the family like strict handling by the parents, sibling jealousy, family disharmony, loss of parent and so on. It is regarded as a symptom of anxiety neurosis.

A stammering child faces tremendous drawbacks in normal development. His inability to express himself forces him to withdraw and become introverted and self-centred. His speech irritates and annoys others and this results in making him feel extremely sensitive and self-conscious. In some cases it may carry a grudge over others and develop intense inferiority complex. He may also try to compensate his handicap by overworking in some other field and asserting his self, and if unsuccessful may revert to anti-social behaviour.

Guidance and Remedy

Speech therapy helps a stammerer to give up faulty habits of articulation and learn how to speak slowly and effectively. Psychotherapy may also help in removing the stress situation in the environment and enable him to have a healthy normal development. Parents and teachers need a lot of patience to bear with the child's sufferings and need to cooperate to provide congenial environment.

2. THE ORTHOPAEDICALLY HANDICAPPED, THE CRIPPLED

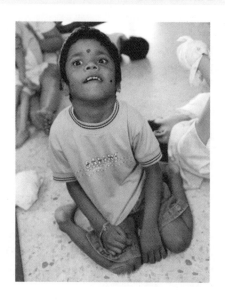 

The causes for the orthopaedically handicapped or crippled may be due to anti-natal deficiencies or various forms of paralysis or serious accidents.

Treatment for the Orthopaedically Handicapped

Today, medical sciences have advanced to such a stage that physical restoration is made possible to the child through orthopaedic surgery and physiological and occupational therapy. Hence, the physical handicap is minimized and results in best physical adjustment of the child.

Guidance and Education

A crippled child not only suffers from physical adjustment but also from emotional and social adjustments. Thus, he requires guidance.

The parental attitudes shown to these crippled children are usually of overprotection or overindulgent nature resulting in children becoming totally dependent on their parents. In some cases, parents reject such children and thus make them feel a sense of guilt and a feeling of anxiety. While in some cases, parents feel humiliated and blame themselves for having given birth to such a child.

The orthopaedically handicapped need psychological support and acceptance from all concerned. Those who cannot be absorbed in regular schools with certain adjustments should be placed in special schools which provide education and training facilities.

Whether the physical handicap is, severe or otherwise, the orthopaedically handicapped needs of an individual are to be studied and treated both medically and psychologically.

3. ORGANIC DISORDERS

(a) Epilepsy

Epilepsy is regarded as an organic disease of the brain. However, the periods prior to and following the epileptic fit are symptomatic of personality or psychological disorder.

At the child guidance clinic they are treated for their psychological and personality disorders than for fits. The idea is that they are made to feel that they are normal and they can continue to study like other children inspite of their handicap. The environmental conditions are made as congenial as possible and all the disturbing factors causing stress are removed.

(b) Endocrinological Imbalance

Endocrinology is comparatively a new science which has shown remarkable progress in pointing out some of the severest personality disorders caused by disturbance of the endocrine balance of the body. The endocrine glands are thyroid, adrenal, pituitary, sex and so on.

The influence of the endocrine glands' secretion is so powerful that in the words of a psychologist, "the so-called higher forms of behaviour are terribly at the mercy of just these lowly secretions especially when something goes wrong with one or more of them."

4. SPECIFIC DISABILITIES

There are certain disabilities which prevent a child from learning the three R's – reading, writing and arithmatic. The child may be otherwise very intelligent but shows little or no progress in scholastic work. These are :

(a) **Congenital dyslexia :** Specific disability in learning to read.

(b) **Congenital dysgraphia :** Specific disability in learning to write.

(c) **Congential apraxia :** Specific disability in learning manual skill.

(d) **Congenital word blindness :** The child is able to see the letter and words distinctly but is unable to interpret the meaning of the written words.

(e) **Congenital word deafness :** The child can hear normally but cannot interpret the meaning of what he hears.

Needs of Physically Handicapped Children

In general, the needs of physically handicapped children are the same as those of other children in the physical, social and emotional areas. They want to run and be active, they want to have fun, they want to be with other people, they want to be loved and accepted and made to feel that they belong. They want to be able to achieve and to be successfull. Unfortunately, a number of these needs are not satisfied. They may need help even in satisfying their basic physical needs. Often these children are rejected or overprotected by their families. Both methods of treatment damage their personalities. They find themselves to be different from the others and are unable to do what normal children can do. All these increase their chances of getting emotionally upset and disturbed.

Intellectually these children require stimulation from the environment just as much as other children do. Those who have problems of sense organs need to learn to compensate for the loss of stimulation from one sensory organ by that received through some other organ. Within their limitations, the handicapped need opportunities to function up to the limits of their capabilities.

A Positive Approach

The emphasis in the upbringing and education of the handicapped is upon what they can do and with providing them with the right experiences. A child should always be prepared for the experience of pain and should be reassured that it is not punishment. In those cases where movement has to be restricted almost completely, steps should be taken to reduce to a minimum, the emptiness of the hours. Moreover, the limitations imposed by physical treatment should be carefully examined in terms of the psychological effect on the child and upon the attitude of the family. The child can be brought to concentrate upon what can be achieved rather than upon the limitations imposed by the disability.

Guidance Education

The psychological guidance of a physically handicapped child and of his family is a delicate and skilled business. Medical skill has a major role to play but it is not the only one. The future of a child depends upon his achievement of personal, social, educational and vocational adjustment at the highest level and throughout. The child and parent need well-informed and sympathetic help. This can be given only by those who are equipped by their training to consider the child as a whole person with needs of the same order as those of normal children.

Many of these children are being sent to special school for the handicapped. All or most of such children need an education with a predominantly manual or vocational content. Yet, among them, are those for whom a more academic and intellectual education is a necessity and who can properly handle later and enter professions for which their disability does not constitute any handicap.

> "When one door of happiness closes, another opens; but often we look so long at the closed door that we do not see the one which has been open for us."
>
> — Helen Keller

III. THE MENTALLY RETARDED

We take the help of intelligence tests of children to measure their mental level of functioning. This is referred to as mental age of the child. When mental age is divided by chronological age and multipled by hundred, Intelligence Quotient (IQ) is calculated. Thus, the measurement of intelligence is popularly known as IQ.

Terman classified children according to IQ as shown below :

Class	Range of IQ
Near genius or Genius	Above 140
Very superior intelligence	120 - 140
Superior intelligence	110 - 120
Normal or Average Intelligence	90 - 110
Dull	80 - 90
Borderline deficiency	70 - 80
Definite feeble-mindedness	Below 70

According to the above table, the mentally deficient could be termed as those having IQ below 70.

However, the International classification of the mentally subnormal, accepted in January 1968, is as follows :

Class	Range of IQ
Borderline	70 - 84
Mild cases (educable)	55 - 69
Moderate (trainable)	40 - 54
Severe	25 - 39
Very severe	Below 25

The classification of intelligence is quite arbitrary and we can find differences of opinion regarding the range of IQ and its corresponding category. The borderline cases are doubtful. They have the chances of being included in the categories of subnormal and normal. But one thing is certain that all mentally retarded or mentally handicapped children possess subnormal intellectual capacities, i.e., they are basically less capable of intelligent behaviour than normal children.

The Characteristics of Mentally Retarded Children

1. They are basically less capable of intelligent behaviour.
2. Their rate of intellectual development is too slow in comparison with children of their own age.
3. They are basically very slow learners.
4. They are very slow and poor in following verbal instructions.
5. They can only understand in terms of concrete objects and situations. So they are very poor at abstraction.
6. They have very poor power of observation, thinking and reasoning.
7. They have difficulty in shifting from one type of activity to another.
8. They are dependent and feel difficulty in managing their affairs themselves.
9. In some cases, the mental deficiency is so great that they are incapable of protecting themselves from dangers.
10. Their interests and aptitudes are very limited.
11. They are essentially incurable in the sense that they cannot get more intelligence through treatment or otherwise. *Mental retardation is not a disease.*
12. Some of them have physical defects. Some of them have vacant looks and clumsy gait. In some cases, they may possess large or small heads.
13. They are socially and emotionally maladjusted.
14. They should not be confused with the persons who are mentally ill or suffer from mental diseases. To make this point clear, the definition given by Wechsler is worth quoting. "Mental deficiency, unlike typhoid fever or general is not a disease. A mentally defective individual is not a person who suffers from a specific disease process but one who, by reason of intellectual arrest or impairment, is unable to cope with his environment to the extent that he needs special care, education and institutionalization."
15. They are deficient in moral judgement. They cannot quite realize what is right and wrong.

Therefore, Who is a Mentally Retarded Person ?

Edgar Doll has given a comprehensive definition to describe who is a mentally retarded person :

"Socially incompetent, i.e., socially inadequate and occupationally incompetent and unable to manage his own affairs at the adult level, mentally subnormal, retarded intellectually from birth or early age, retarded at maturity, mentally deficient as a result of constitutional origin through heredity or disease and essentially incurable."

Causes of Mental Retardation

There could be a number of causes which bring about mental retardation. These are both hereditary and environmental factors.

1. Hereditary (Genetic) Factors

The hereditary factors may be due to the defective genes inherited from either the father or mother. In some cases, the family history of the subnormal usually shows one or the other member mentally defective.

2. Environmental Factors

(a) **Pre-natal causes** : Rh incompatibility, infection during pregnancy, malnutrition, excessive use of drugs, x-rays, sudden shock, quinine, alcohol, smoking, German measles etc.

(b) **Neo-natal causes** : This refers to the conditions which may affect the child during or immediately preceding birth. These include birth injuries such as brain damage, asphyxia, prematurity etc.

(c) **Post-natal causes** : These include factors operative from birth to death. Head injuries during accidents, infections and chronic diseases in early childhood, food deficiencies and malnutrition, socio-cultural and educational deprivation, emotional maladjustment and mental conflicts.

Classification of Mentally Retarded

Since mentally retarded children constitute a heterogenous group it has become necessary to separate them into sub-groups. They include the following sub-groupings :

1. The medical-biological
2. The socio-cultural
3. Classification for educational purposes

Educational Classification for their Education and Training

Children with low intelligence are classified mainly into four groups.

(a) The slow learner (Border line or Dull) : IQ 80 - 90

(b) The educable (Morons) : IQ 55 - 69

(c) The trainable (Imbeciles) : IQ 40 - 54

(d) The totally dependent or profoundly retarded (Idiot) : IQ below 25 - 30

(a) The Slow Learners or Backward Children : (Refer to Page No. 128)

(b) The Educable Mentally Retarded

The educable mentally retarded child is not one who, because of sub-normal mental development, is unable to profit sufficiently from the programme of the regular elementary school but who is considered to have potentialities for development in three areas.

1. Educability in academic subjects of the school at a minimum level.

2. Educability in social adjustment to a point where he can get along independently in the community.

3. Minimal occupational adequacies to such a degree that he can later support himself partially or totally at the adult level.

In most instances, the educable retarded child is not known to be retarded during infancy and early childhood. This retardation and growth in mental and social activities can be noted only if observed closely during the pre-school years. Most of the time the growth is normal and his retardation is not evident until he shows poor learning ability in school.

(c) The Trainable Mentally Retarded

The trainable mentally retarded child is one who is not educable in the sense of academic achievement. Ultimate social adjustment, independence in the community or independent occupational adjustment at the adult level.

The trainable mentally retarded child however, has potentialities for learning :
   (i) Self-help skills
  (ii) Social adjustment in the family and in the neighbourhood
 (iii) Economic usefulness in the home, in school or a workshop

In most instances such children will be known to be retarded during infancy and early childhood. The retardation is generally noted because of known clinical or physical deviations and because the children are markedly delaying in talking and walking.

(d) The Totally Dependent

The totally dependent child is one who because of very severe retardation is unable to be trained in total self-care, socialization or economic usefulness and who needs continued help in taking care of his personal needs. Such a child requires almost complete care and supervision throughout his life since he is unable to survive without help.

There are other classifications.

(a) The National Association for Retarded Children

1. Marginally dependent : IQ 60 - 75

2. Semi-dependent : IQ 25 - 50

3. Dependent : IQ Below 25.

(b) World Health Organization

1. Mild sub-normality : IQ 50 - 69
2. Moderate sub-normality : IQ 20 - 49
3. Severe sub-normality : IQ below 0 - 19.

GUIDANCE, COUNSELLING AND EDUCATION FOR THE MENTALLY RETARDED

The mental subnormality is a great handicap, especially if it is of a severe or a very severe character. The entire development of the infant, i.e., physical, social, emotional along with mental, would be retarded. In very severe cases, the child would not be able to take care of his physique or learn simple habits of walking, toilet training, eating and so on. In other cases, the entire development slows down to such an extent that at times it seems that the child has reached the maximum attainment that it is capable of and parents give up hope of any further improvement. A lot of patience and faith is required to make a retarded infant learn even the basic skills of coordinating the muscles to be able to stand on his feet, crawl by himself, walk, reach out to objects, gain bodily control and so on. Muscular inactivity at times results in extreme restlessness leading to accidents and injury to self. In other words, the individual cannot manage by himself and requires constant supervision, guidance, care and control.

Mental deficiency should be detected early in life to help the child to adjust to his environment before social and emotional problems crop up. Especially in these cases, it has been observed that parents hide the fact that the child is retarded, thinking that it is a God-sent punishment to them. This guilt feeling on their part robs the child of the early care that can be given to him through child guidance clinics, special schools and sheltered institutions. Another problem is that parents refuse to accept the fact that nothing can be done about the low degree of mental ability and move heaven and earth to improve the chances of the child's mental capacity by visiting quacks, taking the child to holy places, or to sadhus who claim to work miracles and so on. Only after breaking their heads, suffering rebuffs, loss of money, energy and time they do realise that they must help the child to make the maximum use of the low ability that he is born with.

The first step in the education of these children is to make their parents realize the truth about their children. They should be persuaded to send their children to the special schools for mentally handicapped children. The schools should be properly managed so that they may provide the essential environment for the maximum development of the personality of the child. Curriculum, methods of teaching and tools for education should be adjusted according to individual needs. Emphasis should be given to co-curricular experiences and they should be given training for manual work and craft. Care should also be taken for their social and emotional development and they should be made able to manage their affairs independently.

The aim of educating these subnormal children is to teach them the art of living, and using their low potential to be able to carry on the routine responsibilities and to be members of the society. The special schools which cater to the needs of these individuals have a curriculum which is entirely concrete in nature, providing maximum freedom to suit each child's mental growth. Instruction is usually individual, rarely in groups. Stress is laid on sensory training and acquisition of perceptual knowledge. Every activity is looked at from its utilitarian aspect to find out whether the child will need to pursue the same later in life. The entire focus is on helping the child to be independent in his physical needs and develop in a manner conducive to his environment so as to minimize behavioural problems. In case of trainable groups, craft becomes the activity, for example, around which the entire instruction is based. Repetition and drill are the watchwards of instruction. For the subnormal can be perfect in a particular activity, if he has drilled it not for days but for months or years. In the case of the educable group who are obviously better than the trainable, simple mental operations (of reading, writing and computation) are introduced in the curriculum. The educable group is given a thorough knowledge and training in how to deal with money transactions and how to carry on simple routine jobs to perfection and precision. The subnormal child is retained in an educational institution for as long as possible in the hope that by being with other children, he will socialise and improve on his personal growth. He is also taught to build relationships and interrelationships with people in his environment, specially his parents and other family members. Care is taken to see that this environment is congenial, pleasing and motivating to help the subnormal child grow socially, emotionally and personally.

It is scientifically proved that a subnormal child seeks greater affection and if not responded to, shows signs of frustration and insecurity. In some cases, it is compensated by excessive eating which results in further physical and physiological problems. As the entire development is delayed, the child learns to communicate with others in the environment rather late. This results in opportunities for expression being thwarted. This has a serious consequence, for the individual may by then develop antisocial behaviour. Similarly, in the case of the retarded, toilet training is delayed, bed-wetting is prolonged, causing further shame in the mind of the family members who cannot entertain their friends as they desire and thus develop a social limitation.

Special schools and classes have sprung up to cater to the educational needs of this group of children. Facilities for training of teachers to deal with the educational, social and emotional problems have been provided. Diagnostic centres have been established to detect the exact degree of mental capacity to put it to maximum use. The appropriate environment for the development of abilities and interests of the retarded has been stressed both at home and at school. With the improvement of psychological tests, retardation is detectable quite early in life thus enabling to segregate these children for better educational facilities, more appropriate to their mental capacity.

IV(A). THE SOCIALLY HANDICAPPED OR DELINQUENTS

The socially handicapped usually include those children who are spoken of as truants, incorrigibles, behaviour problem cases and pre-delinquents and the more seriously maladjusted are the delinquents who if not kept busy today, society should be prepared to be kept busy by them tommorrow.

Causes

It has been proved by different researches in the field of delinquency that delinquent behaviour is a learnt reaction. Delinquents do not inherit delinquent character from their parents or ancestors, but are made so by the uncogenial environmental and social conditions. In this connection, the conclusion drawn by Prof. Udai Shankar is worth mentioning. He writes, "Delinquency is not inherited. It is a product of social and economic conditions and is essentially a co-efficient of the friction between the individual and the community. The most important causes of anti-social behaviour are environmental and sociological in character."

Causes of Delinquency

1. Constitutional or physiological factors

Constitutional factors - like defective constitution or glandular system were offered to explain the cause of delinquent behaviour. Prof. Udai Shankar in his studies also observed that "Poor health, short or too big stature or some deformity which give rise to feeling of inferiority, dispose one to more aggressions, as a compensatory reaction for his inadequacies and consequently one develops delinquent behaviour." Apparently, this alienation seems to be well founded but it is not so. For its support, not much scientific evidence has been reported so far. However, in some cases, it may be taken as one of the causes of delinquent behaviour.

2. Intelligence factor

To put blame on the intellectual deficiency for the delinquent behaviour is also one of the old controversial notions. While earlier writers like Lombroso, Goddard etc., emphasize that the greatest single cause of delinquency and crime is low grade mentality; Burt, Healey, Bronner, Merrill and others strongly deny that delinquents are mentally retarded. In fact, a direct casual relationship between defective intelligence and delinquency is almost doubtful. High intelligence is no guarantee for good behaviour. In many cases, the persons having superior intelligence have been found to be the leaders of notorious gangs and antisocial organizations. Sometimes on the basis of the statistics it is argued that the majority among the delinquents possess low intelligence; therefore, defective intelligence causes delinquency. But this conclusion is not well founded. The collected statistics, in such cases may present an unreal picture. Intelligent individuals may not be caught red-handed where the poor fellows with low intelligence may always be taken in custody. Moreover, defective intelligence may lead to delinquency in one situation and may be a barrier to it in another situation. Therefore, it is not proper to blame low intelligence for the delinquent behaviour.

3. Environmental factors

(a) The home environment

Broken homes, improper parental control, delinquent or criminal behaviour of the parents or other family members, domestic conflicts, economic difficulties, poverty, dull and uninteresting home environment, denial of reasonable freedom and independence to the youngsters, maltreatment and injustice done to the youngsters, make children become victims of emotional problems like inferiority, insecurity, jealousy etc. These make them maladjusted children.

(b) Uncongenial social environment outside the home

The uncongenial home provides the roots for delinquent behaviour, the social environment outside the home nourishes it by supplying some substitutions for the satisfaction of unsatisfied basic needs and urges. For example, the peer group or gang presents itself as a substitute for family love and belongingness. It also satisfies the need of recognition and gives him opportunity for self-dependence and adventure. Anti-social activities of his peer group drags him into anti-social behaviour and persuades him to engage in delinquent acts. Neighbourhood and the places of social contacts and the social situations where the elder members of the society are found engaged in anti-social activities or the mass media like newspapers, books, magazines and cinema that acquaint the children with immoral and antisocial acts, provides serious temptation for the youngsters to become delinquents in order to satisfy their unfulfilled desires and needs.

(c) Maladjustment in the school environment

In many cases of delinquency the uncongenial school environment can be labelled as a stimulating factor. Such uncongenial environment may involve the following elements : defective curriculum, improper teaching methods, lack of co-curricular activities, lack of proper discipline and control, slackness in administration and organization, anti-social or undesirable behaviour of the teachers, maltreatment and injustice done to the child, failure or backwardness.

The foregoing discussion can lead us to conclude that delinquency is an environmental and social disease. Delinquent acts are learnt and acquired. Thus delinquents are not specific types of human beings who are born with some specific innate physical, mental or emotional characteristics. They are quite normal individuals with normal needs and desires, like other normal children, they also want to love, to be loved and to satisfy the need of security, recognition etc. Denial of the satisfaction of these basic needs brings maladjustment and makes them hostile and rebellious.

REMEDY, PREVENTION AND TREATMENT

1. **Parental Education :** Parents should know something about the psychology of delinquency so that they can treat or handle their children properly and provide them with the proper environment for the satisfaction of their basic needs and urges. It requires parental education, help from guidance services, clinics and other voluntary social services can be taken for this purpose.

2. **Save the Child from Bad Company and Anti-social Environment :** Parents, family members and the school authorities should keep a close watch on the activities and social environment of the children and take proper care so that they should not fall into bad company. Some anti-social elements try to hire the youngsters for their own purpose. Attempts should be made to keep children away from their clutches and children should also be made aware of these elements.

3. **Providing Substitutes for a Defective Environment :** Sometimes it is difficult to bring about changes in the defective family environment and also the bad influences of the neighbourhood and peer group. In such cases, children should be removed from their original environment and placed either in foster homes or well-managed reformatories so that they may be provided with a healthy environment for their proper emotional and social adjustment.

4. **To Rectify the School Education and Environment :** The school environment should be made healthy and congenial. The curriculum, methods of teaching, discipline and the social atmosphere of the school be rectified in such a manner that children may not involve themselves in emotional and social maladjustment problems. There is a need of great change in the attitude of those teachers who impose their authority on children and do not try to understand their basic needs. The headmaster as well as the teachers should have a proper knowledge of the psychology of individual differences and delinquency.

CURATIVE MEASURES

The problem of juvenile delinquency is an educational and welfare problem therefore the juvenile delinquents should not be put behind bars and treated like other criminals. Delinquency requires reforms in the form of rehabilitation and re-education and therefore special legal provisions should be made to deal with them. In the progressive communities of the world, legal dealings with juvenile delinquents have been changed. The system of U.K. maintained under "Children's and Young Persons' Act" is worth appreciating. We can adopt it with some essential changes.

Essential features of this system are as follows :

1. Establishment of special juvenile courts with a specially trained magistrate to deal with the juvenile delinquents.

2. Appointment of trained social workers as probation officers for taking charge of delinquent cases.

3. Taking help from clinical psychologists and psychiatrists for understanding the behaviour of the child.

4. Establishment of special schools where the essential provision for education, correction and rehabilitation is possible.

5. Provision of giving the children into custody of fit persons or social agencies.

6. Establishment of Remand Homes where the juvenile delinquents are placed when they wait for their trial or for approved school placement or for being given to the custody of fit persons or as asked by the probation officer.

Provision of a special school or 'approved school' needs special mention in this programme. Such schools have specially trained staff. The curriculum of these schools is flexible and provides opportunities for self-expression, recreation, manual work and learning of useful crafts. Here provisions are made to satisfy the basic needs and urges of the children and thus they are helped in their social and emotional readjustment. In this way the child is helped to get rid of his delinquent behaviour and learn the proper way of responding to social situations and conditions.

In our country also the attitude towards delinquency is changing. In most of the states the "State Children Act" has been enforced and some of them have gone much ahead in the work of rehabilitation and re-education of the young offenders. Separate Child Welfare Boards for dealing with the problem of delinquency has been established and 'approved schools' have come into existence. Some states have encouraged the voluntary organisations to take custody of the delinquent children. Provisions for looking after the neglected and destitute children are also made so that they may not develop into such children. Some states have started foster care programme on the British pattern. Under this programme, the court gives custody of a child to a fit person. Under certain conditions, Remand Homes and appointment of probation officers etc., are also prevalent in many states.

In this way, some efforts are going on to deal sympathetically with the problem of delinquency. But still a good deal remains to be done. States need to take genuine pains in this direction. The greater need, however, is to arouse public consciousness on this problem. No government can solve any social problem without public cooperation. Therefore, there is a need of change in our attitude towards delinquents so that they may be helped in their readjustment and rehabilitation.

IV(B). THE EMOTIONALLY DISTURBED AND MALADJUSTED

The term 'adjustment' refers to a harmonious relationship between the person and the environment through which his needs are satisfied in accordance with social demands. On one hand, if an individual's experiences have so shaped his personality that he is well prepared to play the roles which are expected of him within a given environment and if his basic needs are met by playing such roles then we can say that he is well-adjusted. On the other hand, if experience has not prepared him to play the role of his assigned status or if the environment denies him the normal status for which his experience has prepared him and his fundamental needs are not met, then we say he is 'maladjusted'.

School surveys show us that there is a small group of children who are physically and intellectually normal but because of inherent anomalies of temperament, marked emotional instability or abnormal strength or weakness, even under favourable conditions and often from an early age, are disturbed or maladjusted.

In addition, there are a few who have an organic pathology, the main outward symptoms of which are emotional or behavioural, children with cerebral tumours, cerebral lesions which give rise to excessive activity or other peculiarities.

It is also possible that there are some situations which without prior distortion of development can dramatically give rise to maladjustment, e.g., sudden death of a parent, birth of a younger brother or sister, a scene of adult violence may come at a critical moment in psychological growth and this, if not explained to the child, may bring about serious emotional disturbance. In any situation of difficulty or shock, the temptation is retreat to a previously successful form of behaviour. An individual's acceptance of emotional shock is markedly influenced by constitutional factors, by all that has happened from the moment of birth, by the immediate situation and by the interpretation which the child comes to put upon it.

Usually maladjustment is of slow growth, the result of a series of wrong turnings which bring about disharmony between an individual and the demands of his society. In all such cases the reaction of the individual begins by being normal and the abnormality is in the environment, i.e., when the environment is unsatisfactory and does not provide what a child needs for growth. For example, parental friction, a classic cause for maladjustment in which a child feels insecure because of disunity between his parents by divided loyalties and by fear of aggression or it makes demands which the child's stage of growth is not able to meet. For example, parents insist on exact standards of behaviour, manners at table, quietness in the house or tidiness which are quite beyond the child's power to accomplish. The child can react in different ways; in the first instance the child could become anxious and try to reinforce security by clinging to one parent and in the other instance, the child could show lack of self-confidence or react by aggression. If the situations bringing about such reactions continue, the conflict slowly becomes part of the child's whole unconscious life, affecting his personality even when the provoking situation no longer exists to colour the subsequent emotional life and operate as a factor in determining the future adjustment of the child.

Criteria of Maladjustment

Most of the postulates as to the causes of maladjustment are based upon studies carried out by those whose experience is confined to cases of clearly maladjusted children. But there have been studies which have been made on the basis of comparing abnormal groups with groups of normal children matched for age, sex, level of intelligence and socio-economic levels. These studies indicate that for certain personal factors, signs of maladjustment and environmental influences are significantly more frequent in various types of maladjusted groups but they are not absent from the lives of otherwise normal children. On an average every child shows two or three emotional symptoms.

Moreover, behaviour which at one age is normal may be a sign of maladjustment if it is persisted on when the child grows older, e.g., a tantrum which is normal in the 2 to 3-year-old child but would be a serious sign of maladjustment in a ten-year-old.

Incidence of Maladjustment

It is found that many maladjusted children show very little sign in school to difficulties, but in some, educational retardation itself is not the only obvious sign of maladjustment. Also many children who become retarded in school develop difficulties of personalilty or of behaviour as a consequence of their lack of success. Moreover, maladjustment though it may differ in its forms of expression, is as commonly found among dull and subnormal children as it is among those of superior or normal endowment. Maladjustment is a relative concept and teachers and psychologists are likely to have different views. On one hand, teachers tend to pick out those children who are difficult to manage in class usually because of bad behaviour, poor work, aggressiveness and the like and who are therefore maladjusted that they fail to conform satisfactorily to a classroom situation. Many such children however are passing through a phase of difficulty which is temporary and they readjust without help later. Some may be reacting against the personality of the teacher and the symptoms pass when they move to another class. On the other hand, children whose behaviour is marked by excessive conformity, timidity, shyness or inhibition may escape the teacher's notice or be regarded as model pupils.

Prevention and Remedy

All maladjustment, which is in one way or another mainly the result of interaction with the environment is preventable. The children pathologically abnormal from birth or soon after, can be helped if they are recognized early enough and their parents are assisted in their special need. So also children whose childhood becomes abnormal due to severely disturbing experiences and by their consequences - children who lose their mother in the first two years or who spend long periods in hospital can be protected from the worst consequences of deprivation or shock.

V. THE GIFTED CHILDREN

One day a partially deaf lad was given a note from his teacher to give his mother, suggesting that she take him out of school, because he was too stupid to learn.

The mother's reaction was to set to it, and began teaching him herself. The boy grew up, and Thomas Edison, for that was his name, left a wealth of inventions that leaves us all deeply in his debt.

He invented the motion picture, the record player, and the light bulb. When he died, the U.S. as a nation switched off all electric lights for one minute in his memory, at a time decided on at the national level.

WHO ARE GIFTED CHILDREN ?

The gifted children are the exceptionally clever children who can be classified as those possessing IQ 140 and above and referred to as near genius or genius. They possess unusual abilities which are not accessible to everybody.

In the words of Havighurst, "The talented or gifted child is one who shows consistently remarkable performance in any worthwhile line of endeavour."

While Prem Pasricha has given the following definition for the gifted child :

"The gifted child is the one who exhibits superiority in general intelligence or the one who is in possession of special abilities of high order in the fields which are not necessarily associated with high intelligence quotient."

The Characteristics of Gifted Children

(*i*) The gifted children are the exceptionally clever children.

(*ii*) They possess IQ 140 and above.

(*iii*) They are referred to as near genius or genius.

(*iv*) They possess unusual abilities which are not accessible to everybody.

(*v*) In comparison to children of their own age group, they are superior in some ability or group of abilities.

(*vi*) In most of the cases, the gifted children always exhibit superior performance in the area, or areas of their giftedness only.

(*vii*) The gifted children include not only the academically talented but also those who show promise in :

    (*a*) Music, dance, drama, painting, sculpture, writing and other creative arts.

    (*b*) Mechanical work.

    (*c*) Social leadership and human relationships.

    (*d*) Creative scientific experimentation and exploration.

    (*e*) Physical activities like games, sports and gymnastics.

(*viii*) On receiving proper attention and opportunity for self-expression and development, they can contribute something remarkable to the welfare of their society, nation and humanity at large.

HOW TO IDENTIFY THE GIFTED CHILDREN ?

For adequate identification of the children who are gifted, the teacher must make a proper distinction between the intellectually gifted and children with special talent who show superior performance in some area or the other. In the identification of the intellectually gifted, intelligence tests are often used. An IQ of 140 or above is usually accepted as the most agreeable criteria for identifying the gifted child.

De Haan and Kough have provided a list of identifying characteristics which can be of great help. According to them, a gifted child :

1. Learns rapidly and easily.
2. Uses a great deal of commonsense and practical knowledge.
3. Reasons things out, thinks clearly, recognizes relationships and comprehends meanings.
4. Retains what he has heard or read without much rote drill.
5. Knows about many things of which most students are unaware.
6. Has a large vocabulary which he uses easily and accurately.
7. Can read books which are one or two years in advance of the rest of the class.
8. Performs difficult mental tasks.
9. Asks many questions and has wide range of interests.
10. Does some academic work, one or two years in advance of the rest of the class.
11. Is original in his thinking, uses good but unusual methods.
12. Uses both divergent and convergent thinking to solve the problems.
13. Is alert, keenly observant and responds quickly.

There are some gifted children who do not possess superior general intelligence but exhibit special abilities in one or the other fields. Such type of children need careful observation and study so that their specific talents can be spotted out. Aptitude test, anecdotal reports of friends and teachers often help in exploring the special giftedness of children. Such children need encouragement. Wise and expert teachers should try to use the specific abilities and talents of the children.

The Needs and Problems of the Gifted Child

Need for security, a sense of belonging, and need to be accepted as an individual.

They also have a few special needs like :

1. The need for knowledge and understanding.
2. The need for creativity.
3. The need for the development of his exceptional ability.
4. The need for self-actualisation and self-expression or self-fulfilment.

The gifted child not only shines for the satisfaction of his basic needs but also needs the opportunity and facilities for the realisation of his special needs.

If these needs are not satisfied, the child may be emotionally and mentally disturbed.

The gifted child needs a proper environment for his development. He wants to be understood. He is exceptionally curious and has a thirst for knowledge. Therefore, he has the habit of asking searching questions. Parents and teachers who do not understand him, snub him. Sometimes he wants appreciation for his creativity but does not get it. Consequently he feels insecure and rejected. Mishandling or carelessness on the part of the teacher or parents further aggravates the situation and he turns into a nuisance.

Reasons for the Gifted Child's Maladjustment

In case a gifted child gets undue attention and appreciation he becomes conscious of his superiority and develops a boastful attitude. He cannot adjust with the other students. He thinks of them to be inferior or foolish. On the other hand, the other children become jealous of such a child and they do not accept the superiority and begin to reject him. This makes him quite perturbed and he turns into a withdrawn personality and becomes aggressive and hostile.

Lack of opportunities and appropriate environment will also result in maladjustment in gifted children.

In our usual system of classroom education, the gifted children face a number of adjustment problems. Teachers plan work for the average child. This provides no challenge for the gifted child and he finishes it in no time or takes no genuine interest in it. As a result he becomes restless, inattentive, careless and idle. He often utilizes his entire time and surplus energy in mischief and creating problems of discipline in the classroom and out of school. Taking into consideration all these problems, there is a need for special care and proper education for the gifted child.

Education of the Gifted Child

There is an urgent need of a well-thought-out programme or scheme of special education for the gifted children. The following plans have been put forward by different thinkers for providing education for the gifted :

1. **Separate schools**   2. **Separate classes**
3. **Double promotion**   4. **Enrichment programme**

It is often suggested that we have separate schools for the gifted children and adequate facilities should be provided in these schools. Such segregation is often criticized and labelled as undemocratic. The students educated from these schools develop an aristocratic and concerted attitude and in this way try to widen the gulf between educated and uneducated or privileged and under privileged.

Similarly, the segregation of the gifted children into separate section within the same school has the same danger. This plan is known as ability grouping. Here a given grade is divided into different sections on the basis of ability. The non-feasibility of both these plans involving segregation is obvious in the Indian context. We cannot afford such segregation and it cannot bring about any fruitful results.

Another concept in the education of the gifted children is double promotion. This plan although quite feasible suffers from a serious defect. It creates a gulf between educational ability and experience. They also have adjustment problems with the children who are senior to them in age. Though intellectually at par with them, they lag behind emotionally, socially and physically, and thus become victims of adjustment problems.

We will now consider the enrichment programme for the gifted children. This consists in the selection and organisation of learning experiences and activities appropriate to the child's adequate development. In this way the enrichment of education should be considered a need of all students. But in the case of gifted children it will definitely imply an urgent need. Enrichment programmes aim to give additional educational opportunities for the gifted children. It may include :

1. Special assignments that can be within the syllabus or outside the syllabus.
2. Work on independent projects.
3. Preparing reports and participation in panel discussion.
4. Independent library reading.
5. Visits to places for getting first hand information.
6. Construction of models and teaching aid material.
7. Participation in the organisation of co-curricular activities.
8. Experimentation and independent research.
9. Helping the students who need additional help.
10. Giving leadership.

Enrichment programmes provided in the school is the most suitable plan for the education of gifted children. It does not only provide facilities for the full development of the special abilities and potentialities of the child but also cares for the development of his total personality. Such a programme is beneficial to both the average and the gifted. Both can develop according to their own abilities and capacities without interfering in the development of others.

Home Adjustment of the Gifted Child

Too often, parents who have discovered that their child has the ability far beyond than those of other children of his age emphasise this fact to the detriment of the child. When friends visit the home, the child is called upon to exhibit his special but still untrained talent. The child will certainly be affected by this experience. After a while he may no longer desire to be the family entertainer. He may develop an attitude of resentment. Evidence of superiority in a child should be recognized but not overemphasized.

The gifted show signs of leadership. They expect other children to be interested in the games that they want to play and to the rules that they establish. This aggressiveness can be sometimes traced to parental over-encouragement of self-expression. This leads the child to many adjustment handicaps when he enters school. The problems of the gifted child that arise in the home multiply as he passes into high school. Since he is able to progress through school more rapidly than pupils of average ability he may begin early to demand privileges that the parents consider too advanced for his age. Inspite of the fact that the parents have encouraged him in his rapid school progress, his parents realize that he is just a child. They believe that it is wise to deny him the liberties that his more mature classmates are enjoying. The parents' inability to explain to them satisfactorily the reasons for their attitude often causes conflict in the home and great unhappiness for the children.

However, if the child is permitted to participate in the desired social activities, he discovers that he must be one of the group. An intellectually superior but emotionally and socially immature young person may have difficulty in making a satisfactory adjustment to the attitude and behaviour of his chronologically older and emotionally more mature classmates.

The specially talented young person presents a different problem. In their relations with him, other persons may tend to emphasise his special aptitude to the neglect of other desirable qualities that he may possess. Hence, he may develop the attitude that he is good for only one thing. Also this young person develops a keen desire to gain success in his field of talent and other adjustment problems are shunted aside. The school cannot overcome the handicap that originated at home. His parents want this special success to continue, consequently the individual creates adjustment problems for himself as it becomes difficult for him to live with his family.

Guidance for the Gifted Children

Gifted children stand out, and therefore, require a special treatment or else they fall into apathy and boredom. The most appropriate way of handling these children is to permit them to lead others or to be leaders of the group.

It is very easy for the teachers to spot out these outstanding pupils. They show mastery in one or more fields and easily take on airs of superiority towards their classmates. If this condition is not recognised either by the teacher or other classmates, the child begins to get restless and disturbed and takes to mischief or unhealthy attitudes. To save him on time, the teacher must accept his mental superiority and give him the position of a leader. In other words, gifted children have to be separated from the bulk and given responsible position of leading others.

The most important question is, how can a teacher train the few gifted ones to develop leadership qualities ?

The chief criterion is the high general ability of the individual. The higher the intelligence, the more receptive will the pupil be to developing initiative, co-operation, sociability, independability and a sense of humour.

There are three decisive ways of helping these pupils.

(i) **Achievement motivation :** The leader should be motivated to achieve the highest possible strength to reach the maximum of which he is capable. He should be led through moderate risks and should be ready to face them. He must be eager to succeed and persist in the activity even in case of failure. He should never feel content with his performance and should be ready for mobility, flexibility and adventure. Above all, he should be ever active and value every moment of time.

(ii) **Concept of influence in the group :** A leader should have a hold on the group and this he has to acquire through training. It is through group discussions and leadership camps that the leader learns the techniques of persuasion, how to press a point and convince the group. Lectures on leadership and group dynamics are also of immense use.

(iii) **Character formation :** A strong will-power, selfless dedication, single-mindedness, fortitude, facing reverses with a strong stand, and a sense of participation are some of the character traits, the leader has to possess. These can be acquired through talks and dialogues. Especially important is the adolescent stage, to conceive dreams of high ideals of life, to imbibe high principles of conduct and govern one's life by them.

"Educate the whole child. Don't get so wrapped up in your subject matter that you forget the child infront of you."

— Sister Mary Fortunata, SND

CHAPTER 11

CHARACTER FORMATION IN CHILDREN

Thomas and Nancy Lincoln lived in a one-room log cabin in Kentucky's wilderness. Mr. Lincoln was a hunter, but an extremely poor man. In this cabin Sarah was born in the year 1807 and two years later her brother Abraham, the future President of the United States of America.

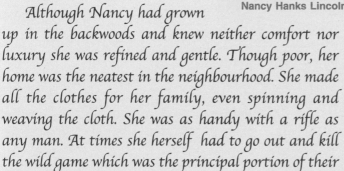

Nancy Hanks Lincoln

Thomas Lincoln

Although Nancy had grown up in the backwoods and knew neither comfort nor luxury she was refined and gentle. Though poor, her home was the neatest in the neighbourhood. She made all the clothes for her family, even spinning and weaving the cloth. She was as handy with a rifle as any man. At times she herself had to go out and kill the wild game which was the principal portion of their diet. She could wield an axe and a hoe. Often neighbours saw her in the field clearing the land and working.

Abraham Lincoln

Their cabin had no floor, only the bare earth, tramped level and hard. There was no door, and practically no furniture. A square hole in the wall was their sole window.

IN THIS UNPROMISING PLACE GREW UP ABRAHAM LINCOLN, one of the greatest men of all times. His mother was one of the few pioneers who could read and write. By the light of the fire - (they could not afford candles) - she read to Sarah and Abraham from the one book in their home, the Bible. From it, mother Lincoln taught her children to read and spell. There were no schools ; only an occasional travelling teacher, who would stop in a settlement for a few weeks to instruct everyone, adult as well as child. There Lincoln began the training of *MIND, WILL* and *HEART* that made him the outstanding man that he became.

"One cannot always be a hero, but one can always be a man."

- Johann W. Goethe

WHAT IS CHARACTER ?

"The crown and glory of life is character. It is the noblest possession of man, constituting a rank in itself, an estate in general good will; dignifying every station, and exalting every position in society.

It exercises a great power than wealth and secures all the honour without the jealousies of fame.

It carries with it an influence which always tells; for it is the result of proved honour, rectitude and consistency, qualities which perhaps more than any others, command the general confidence and respect of mankind."

— Samuel Smiles

Right from the time of conception, the environmental forces within the mother's womb and outside influence the character of the child. The family is the first social institution where the foundation stone regarding the character of the child is laid down. Outside the family, the neighbourhood, community and the social forces influence the character of the child. Once he steps into the school, the whole school environment influences the formation of character. Parents and teachers have the greatest role in the formation of character of children.

A school going child spends most of his time in the school. Therefore, his teachers, classmates, the whole school curriculum with its curricular and co-curricular activities mould the character of the child. It is said, **"Character development is the greatest, if not the sole, aim of education."**

— O'Shea

Therefore at every stage, in any system of education, character development is regarded as one of the important aims of education. Both parents and teachers need to work together for the greatest task of character development in children.

"Character building — the task of a life time — demands the richest spiritual materials; faith, courage, humility, integrity, magnanimity, nobility, self-abnegation. Wealth, influence, position, power - these are of little value without character. Grandeur of character is the moral principle in practice."

— Grenuille Kleiser

HOW WE CAN BUILD THE CHARACTER OF CHILDREN ?

1. Proper Training of Instincts and Emotions

Instincts form the rock-bottom of character. Therefore, the first step in the formation of character is the sublimation and modification of instincts. Instincts and emotions give birth to so many elements of one's character. Nature of instinctive and emotional behaviour contributes much to the character development. Therefore, proper care should be taken to modify and sublimate the instinctive impulses and emotions along socially desirable channels. For example, the instinct of children to fight and the emotion of anger can be channalised into good deeds and thus help in character formation.

"Remember, the school is only as good as its teachers. You are the soul, the life of the school".

— Sister Mary Bernarda, SND

2. Organization of Good Habits

Sow an act and you reap a habit ;
Sow a habit, and you reap a character ;
Sow a character and you reap a destiny.

— Jeremy Taylor

Habits form a path of the character. Therefore, when children are young, due care should be taken to develop healthy habits among children. For example, waking up in the morning, regular eating habits, doing homework, being truthful etc.

3. Training of Willpower

"Character is not in the mind. It is in the will."

— Fulton J. Sheen

There is a perfect correlation between will and the character. Proper care should be taken for the development of a strong willpower among the children. Firm determination to work for a good cause and the power of taking the right decision at a right time are products of will. These two qualities are very essential for the development of a strong character. Mahatma Gandhi and his struggle to get freedom for India is a good living example of willpower and the strength of character. Those who have good willpower are persons of strong character. A man of strong will can make himself free from the harmful factors and can overcome all the obstacles in life and be a man of character. Thus says, Boenchim, **"When we talk of a strong character we mean strength of will."**

4. Development of Proper Sentiments

"Sentiment is a more or less permanent and organized system of emotional tendencies and impulses centred about some object or person."

— Valentine

Character is referred to as the system or organization of sentiments. Therefore, care should be taken to develop a well organized stable system of healthy sentiments among the children.

To quote MeDougall, "The units of character are the sentiments and thus asserts that character is the system or organization of sentiments."

Therefore, first of all due consideration should be paid for developing the right type of sentiments – sentiments like; patriotism, love and brotherhood, moral sentiment, social sentiment, intellectual sentiment, cultural sentiment, aesthetic sentiment and self-regarding sentiment. Later on, all these positive sentiments should be well organized with the help of the Master sentiment, i.e., the Self-regarding Sentiment. The strength of one's character always depends upon the sentiment of Self-regard or Master sentiment.

Therefore, children must be helped to develop a strong sense of self-respect and a sentiment of self-regard. The following points will help in developing the Master sentiment or Self-regarding sentiment in children :

(a) Consider each child as a unique being.

(b) Each child has his God-given talents and capabilities.

(c) Each child has his right to develop himself as a worthwhile person.

(d) Due respect must be shown for the individuality of the child.

(e) Each child should be given reasonable freedom in day-to-day work.

(f) He must be encouraged to do his work independently.

(g) He must get love, acceptance and emotional security to become a self-confident person.

(h) He must be encouraged to share and play a role of a responsible citizen at home, school and in society.

So character is the organized self of instincts, emotions, habits, attitudes, temperament, intellect, motivation, will, self-image and sentiments. The study of one's character needs complete understanding of many other factors affecting his total personality.

5. Parents, Teachers and Other Elders as Role Models

Children are imitative by nature. They imitate whatever they see and hear. For a child, parents, teachers and elders are role models. He imitates them consciously and unconsciously. Therefore, they should place the ideal examples of their own conduct and character. Children must be provided a healthy and inspiring atmosphere at their homes and in their schools.

6. Children are Suggestive

Just like imitating, children are very receptive to suggestions. So, suggestion plays an important role in the formation of good character. One must make sure that positive suggestion is given to children for bringing desirable behaviour in them. This can be achieved through ideal stories and life sketches of great men and women who had a great impact in the social, cultural, spiritual, moral patriotic, and scientific aspects of a society. Children should be given a word of praise for their satisfactory progress. Auto-suggestion can also bring very good results in children.

7. Socialization of the Child

Social development is a part of character. A socially developed child always behaves according to the norms and values of the society, and therefore is more conscious of his character. He must be helped in the inculcation of desirable social virtues, life cooperation, teamspirit, tolerance, forgiveness, understanding etc., so that he can maintain a healthy relationship with his peers and other members of the society.

8. Development of Worthy Ideals

The character of a person can be judged through his values and ideals. Higher the ideals and goals of life, the stronger is the character of a person. Therefore, children should be made to develop worthy ideals, higher values and noble aims of life so that they can build a better world.

9. Proper Mental Development of the Child

Intellect plays a vital role in the organization of the elements of character. Each and every person has to make lots of adjustments in his life according to the situations and circumstances. Life is full of challenges. How a person will behave in a particular situation and face the realities of life depends upon his intellectual powers. Therefore, proper care should be given to develop the intellectual powers like reasoning, thinking, imagination, discipline, concentration and socializing.

10. The Role of Religion and Moral Education in Character Development

Religious and moral education have a greater role in the character formation of children. Religious instructions will help children to understand and respect each and every religion. It helps to develop the values of tolerance, love and brotherhood, forgiveness and above all; that all are equal infront of God and He has created each one in His own image. Further, moral education will help children to develop many social values. Therefore, no one can question the utility of moral and religious education as an instrument for character formation.

11. Praise and Reproof

Reward and punishment both occupy an important role in the development of character. In this age, the role of punishment in character formation is decried. So lighter terms like disciplinary action or a positive action for improvement in character could be used since we cannot give up the corrective measure completely in our educational system. So along with measures of rewards, praise, appreciation and other methods for due incentive and encouragement, certain corrective measures or disciplinary actions are needed when things really go wrong, for proper character development of children.

12. Healthy Competition

Healthy competition is a motivating factor for character formation. In a healthy competition the individual competes with his own past record.

The other factors which would help in the character formation of children are instilling in them the values of co-operation, team spirit, self-discipline and hardwork.

"There is no curriculum or method that will produce character by magic. On the contrary, every experience in the home, at church, on the playground or at school presents an opportunity for character development. "

— Skinner and Harriman

CHAPTER 12

ADOLESCENTS

LETTER TO GIRLS AGED 11 AND ABOVE

Dear Ananya and Friends,

This is a letter for all the girls of age 11 and above.

You are entering a New Exciting and Wonderful world - the world of the teenager. You'll find that a lot of the girls you make friends with will feel that they are completely grown up and in some ways they are. And you, yourself, are rushing into the physical and emotional you that you'll be all your life.

Don't worry about the signs of departing childhood. They can be worrying because they are strange. But they are also very wonderful. You must be proud that these things are a part of you. Sometimes, like everyone else, you probably wonder why you are here at all! Whatever your destiny may be, one thing is absolutely certain! You are here, as a human female, to be a link in the chain of life. From the moment you were born you became tremendously important to Nature and to the whole human race.

This is because you were given THE POWER TO CREATE LIFE. The seeds of this marvellous mechanism were there at the time of your birth, and indeed before it. Now you are beginning to have a proof of this.

Try to keep in mind always that every change and activity in your mind and body are a part of this life - a gift just to you. They are personal and intimate, something you can treasure for yourself, but that doesn't mean having a sort of guilty secret. It is something to be proud of, and dignified about.

Don't imagine, because you sometimes feel disturbed at the changes you notice that you are different from any other girl, or from your mother or any grown up woman you know. Every girl at the onset of puberty feels like this. The only danger is to be frightened because you are ignorant or don't really understand what you have been told.

Two things will be terribly important to you very soon, or they may already be happening. The first is the development of your breasts. These days, as you will see in the advertisements in magazines, breasts are regarded as very important features of a woman's attractiveness. As in so many matters, there can be a lot of silly affectation about the size of the bust, but men's admiration for a lovely bosom and a woman's pride in it are right and natural. They indicate an instinctive regard for a woman's feminity - that gift of life.

Your breasts are created for one most important purpose: to feed the babies, hope you will have. In the wall of your chest are two glands. Since you were born they have remained small - as small indeed, as in your brother. Now, as you know, they have been growing rapidly, and they will continue to develop through your teens as Nature prepares you for motherhood.

Some girls feel miserable because their breasts are small, but if you are worried because at the moment you have no reason to wear a bra, just be patient. Your breasts will go on developing for some years.

Other girls have big breasts, and they get so embarrassed that they hunch their shoulders and slouch in an endeavour to disguise the curves. Once one teenager remarked, that she felt like cutting off her breasts because she found her breasts too large. The idea of large is usually imagined, just because the development of their bust is new and strange. But a comfortable, nicely - shaped bra can make any girl's breasts look firm and well proportioned. And if yours are really rather large at first, your body will soon grow up to them so to speak.

Remember, a young woman with a lovely bosom is every famous artist's or sculptor's delight.

Just as Nature gets you ready for womanhood by developing your breasts to nourish your future babies, so she busies herself on the much more wonderful and intricate mechanism which will enable you to create those babies. Since your generation has been given a diet and general care better than that of any girl in the past, your body is able to get on with this job earlier than used to be the case.

That is why you may start having periods by your 11th birthday or even earlier or later. But whenever this happens - and nobody knows exactly when it will happen - you will feel quite happy about it if you understand why it occurs at all.

You probably don't know that when you were born your body contained about 30,000 eggs. They were there at the start and you have not created any since, nor will you ever do so.

In theory you could have thirty thousand babies! But this is obviously only a theory, but Nature is lavish just to make sure. You know how gardeners sow hundreds of seeds in a garden just to get a few plants.

Anyway these eggs are stored away in your ovaries which are tucked away in what you might (inaccurately) call your tummy. The eggs are kept safe and sound in a tiny bed, rather like a cocoon but infinitely small.

Now as you are growing up, the eggs begin to move and develop. At the end of its journey each egg has increased enormously in size but it is still only a one hundred and-twentieth part of an inch in diameter, if you can imagine anything so small. At the end of the journey there is a sort of seed-bed rich in nourishment, soft and damp-which is called a membrane. As the egg is the germ of human life the seed-bed has nourishing blood on which the egg can feed.

After you are married the time will come, when this egg will be fertilized and remain in the seed-bed, developing over nine months into a baby.

But for years to come there will be no reason for the egg to stay there. After a while it will be dislodged, together with the membrane, or seed-bed. And then you have a period.

Usually this happens about every 28 days, but until your body has adapted itself to this important and wonderful rhythm of moving an egg on its journey and setting it in the membrane, the interval may vary greatly.

My dear friends, this is a simple explanation of a menstrual period. There is nothing to be frightened of or ashamed of. This is not anything impure and unclean. But an awful lot to marvel at.

Accept that your periods, like your breast development, are proofs of your health and growth. Of course, they are private, personal matters which you will want to keep to yourself. But if anything about them worries you, don't suffer in silence. Talk to your Mother or your Teacher. They were, once, girls just like you.

An Adolescent's Reflection

Are you my friend, God,

a real friend I can count on ?

A true, honest friend who will stand by me,

and not be put off by my acting out ?

If so,

I want to talk to you today —

about myself, my world, my friends,

the endless questions I have,

the hundred and one things we need to talk about,

and the things I never tell anyone.

LETTER TO BOYS AGED 13 AND ABOVE

*D*ear Ashish and Friends,

 This is a letter addressed to all the boys of age 13 and above.

To begin with, don't be impatient to grow up too quickly in the New Exciting World - the world of the teenager. Nature has her programme and won't be hurried by wishful thinking, bad temper or grumbling. And galling as it may be, boys have to accept the fact that in the journey to Adulthood they come second to girls. The signs that indicate a boy becoming a man come later than those for a girl. So don't get worried if your sister is very obviously growing up, or even if she seems to be losing interest in the games that you still like.

Just to reassure you that you are no different from other boys, whatever they may boast, you will probably move from boyhood to adolescence between thirteen and fifteen. That's when there begins what a doctor or your biology teacher would call 'the secondary sexual characteristics'. It's all a matter of glands. The gland which busies itself in making you male produces a secretion called a hormone which goes into your blood stream and then gets to work to complete the year - long task of making you an adult man.

As a matter of fact, these hormones have been pouring into your blood since you were about ten years old. They haven't had much obvious effect - beyond making you tougher and rougher, and possibly what the grown -ups call 'moody'. May be you shouldn't be knowing this because you could answer any complaints about 'not being the nice little boy you used to be' by blaming it on those hormones!

However, it is true enough that some of your changes of mind, your sudden boredom with hobbies and games you once liked, your enthusiasm for new activities, and those blotches and pimples on your face, are signs that you too are nearing that exciting time called adolescence.

Frankly, it will be some time yet before you can ever pretend there is any hair on your face to shave, but I expect there are signs of hair on your body. Body hair develops mostly in areas where the friction of adjacent areas of skin could cause soreness and movement causes sweat which needs to be soaked up. Any bewilderment you may have because you seem to be still a boy in body but have disturbing thoughts which hint that your mind is rushing ahead. You have worked out the situation perfectly correctly. Your mind is indeed changing. It is preparing itself for your older body and because mental development can be quicker than physical changes you are bound to be worried.

You, and every boy who ever was, are bound to experience a new sort of dream. The old nightmare of bogymen, pursuing lions, and big black growling dogs, or the nice dreams of lots of sweets and toys, will change to disturbing, vague and yet stimulating dreams you will not be able to recall with any exactitude when you wake up. And they may well have a physical effect on you. Your sex organs will be affected and you'll be aware of them when you wake up.

Long ago they had silly ideas about all this, feeling it must be wrong. It's one reason why, if you read books about schools in the old days, there is a lot about getting up very early, having cold baths, and indulging in exhausting exercises.

Nowadays we know the dreams and half-awake thoughts a boy has aren't wrong, though like everything else in life, they must be controlled, rather than suppressed.

The best thing would be that you try to accept your dreams, your occasional feelings of despair, your bursts of energy when you feel tempted to be a young savage, and even those spots on your face, as part of your life for the time being.

Don't brood on them, and if they get too much for you, discuss them with your father, your teacher, or any man you really like. Remember, they once had your problems.

You are curious about girls, about babies, how they are made and where they come from. But your curiosity about yourself doesn't really extend to the fact that you personally, will one day be as directly involved in love and babies as any girl. That's a clue to show that you are still on the young side. Don't force your mind to probe into all this sex business just to be a know-all. Don't listen to those boys who want to whisper a lot of nonsense about it - ten to one they have got it all mixed up or have just picked up some unpleasant stories which will leave you feeling unclean and rather sick after you have listened to them.

Don't bother to read the dirty books, which are sometimes passed from hand to hand at school. They are rather like wallowing in a muddy pool - you wouldn't do that if you could swim in a clean fresh sea. In fact the boys who get their knowledge of sex this way are usually those who have old-fashioned parents who don't tell them the truth.

Someday, you will realize that you are going personally to contribute to this wonderful adventure of being a human being. That's when you'll need to know the real facts about yourself as someone you'll love in a sexual way.

Be patient, you are growing up, you are slowly but inevitably becoming a man. In the meantime, don't be ashamed at being a real boy and don't be restless because time passes slowly. And above all, YOU ARE THAT IMPORTANT PERSON - THE HUMAN MALE.

These days you must have been hearing about Homosexuals or Gay people getting married etc. You may have even asked to each other about who they are and what they are. Here is a simple explanation about who they are.

HOMOSEXUALITY may be defined as an attraction towards the same sex. Eg. Boys being attracted to boys are referred as 'Gay". The general behaviour is that the boys are attracted towards girls and this is natural. Due to certain psychological deviations, some boys may be attracted towards the same sex. This is certainly a deviant behaviour. The Gay people are fighting for their rights and you may have read in the newspapers that gay men are getting married to each other also. This is against natural behaviour of the human beings. For e.g. If a person has only one upper limb and the other limb is missing from birth, he is certainly not "normal" though we show compassion on him to lead as normal a life as possible. He cannot be classified as " normal" because he will have certain handicaps or difficulties as compared to others. Similarly gay men cannot be classified as "normal" but should be shown compassion as their deviant behaviour from the normal is probably not by choice, but due to any of a variety of psychological disorders and circumstances. Gay men are known to be more violent in their reactions and behaviour when compared to other men. AIDS was first detected among gay men and later it was found that it can also occur in other people. As the society does not consider 'gay" behaviour as normal, these men tend to hide their behaviour from society and many of the diseases are not brought to the notice of the doctor.

Boys of your age will want to try out new things in life. You must remember the story of Pandora's box, which was opened out of curiosity. Though it is natural to be curious, it could be dangerous to experiment. You should certainly avoid even trying out smoking, alcohol, drug (which are used to produce excitement and enhance the moods or to feel good), etc. as you could become a slave to the habit or can develop physical addiction to the chemical leading to injury to physical and mental health. Your parents or teachers can guide you if there are any problems that you are facing.

You must remember that adolescence is a difficult period in many as you are confused about most of the things happening within and around you. You should be ready to share any of your feelings with your parents or teachers. They will understand you and help you to overcome the difficult period.

An Adolescent's Reflection

I am pulled in so many directions ;

I feel like a bundle of contradictions.

I feel like a child at times –

but want to be treated like a grown-up,

I fear being treated like a grown-up,

and want to be looked after,

almost like a child.

I want to be sure that I count,

that my life is worth living.

Be my friend always, and help me to believe in myself,

and in life.

Help me to learn from others' mistakes and from my own

and to admit my failures.

Do not let me waste my youth in selfish and idle pursuits.

Teach me to rather use these years

to learn who I am, and what I want.

TEENAGERS' CLUB

Brian aged 16 says, "My mother irritates me, she treats me like a little boy. When I sneeze once she thinks I'm sick. My mother likes to play the doctor role and she makes me sick. My mother hovers over me like a mother-hen and I'm fed up with her concern. I think I'm entitled to sneeze without an explanation."

Fig. 12.1. Teenagers' sharing

While Michelle says, "My father doesn't love me any more from the time my younger brother was born."

Says Rahul, "My father is sensitive to temperature but not to temperament.

He is totally unaware of emotions and moods. He talks but doesn't communicate."

Nikhil says, "My father is unable to feel close to people. His talk is never person to person, it is always station to station. He judges in advance."

While Ranjit says, "My mother doesn't converse, she lectures. She turns the simplest idea into a complex inquiry. I ask a short question, she gives me a long answer. I avoid her. Her speeches take too much of my time. I wish she talked in sentences and paragraphs, not in chapters."

Jim says, "I'm sick and tired of my father's advice; he always talks about my future. In the meantime he is ruining my present. I've no confidence in myself. I feel like a failure."

Says Lara, "My mother puts her nose into everything I do. She comes to check in my room. She even checks my phone calls. To whom I've talked etc... etc. She is so overprotective and she never lets me go to my friend's house alone."

Rehan, past 18, says "My dad never allows me to drive his car while my friends drive their own to college."

Pat 17 years says, "My mother has no respect for me. She invades my privacy and violates my civil rights. She comes to my room and rearranges my drawers. She can't stand disorder," she says, "I wish she'd tidy up her room and leave mine alone. I deliberately mess up my desk as soon as she cleans it up. But my mother never learns."

Denis, "My teacher is so slow. Her voice is so monotonous. And we have her for two periods, maths and science one right after the other."

Jack, "We had a literature class but we chose to read comic books while he continued his own style of lecturing."

Well, it goes on ....and on .... among the vibrant and challenging teenagers.

PARENTS' CORNER

Parent-"My relationship with my son is a tragedy of errors. I am his friend.

He considers me his enemy. I want his respect, but I get his contempt."

Parent-"When we stress on modest dress, she wears tight and low waist jeans. She wears summer clothes in winter."

Parent-"When we encourage good literature he'll fill our home with comic books."

Parent-"When we stress a balanced diet, he goes for fast food and ice cream.

He takes lots of coffee and soft drinks. We are concerned about his health."

Parent-"If we encourage grace and good manners, he is rude in speech and uses slangs. When we correct him, he becomes rebellious."

Parent-"When we stress on physical exercises he refuses to exercise. He lies on the sofa and watches various channels on the T.V. for long hours."

Parent-"If we value neatness, he becomes sloppy, his room messy, and his clothes repulsive and his hair unkept and long. When we treasure peace and good neighbourly relationships he'll quarrel with our neighbours, tease their dogs and bully their children."

Parent-"When we stress on academic standards, he will sink to the bottom of the class."

Parent-"When we call our daughter for the family meal together, she becomes moody and goes under the blanket and refuses to talk."

Parent-"Our son's moods fluctuate. It is sad to see his annoying mannerisms such as; nail-biting, finger-drumming, feet-tapping, throat-clearing or grimacing."

Parent-"When we worry about air pollution and lung cancer, he will smoke like a chimney."

Fig. 12.2. Parents' sharing

PARENTS are often at a loss as to how to relate to their teenagers, yet they want to continue to be involved in their teen's lives. They understand the importance of staying connected, but sometimes feel frustrated and discouraged by the obstacles they face.

Adolescence is a time of turmoil, stress and storm. Rebellion against authority and against convention is to be expected and tolerated for the sake of learning and growth.

The adolescence of children is a difficult time for parents. It is not easy to watch a pleasant child turn into an unruly adolescent. It is sad to see him nail-biting, squinting, stammering, stuttering, sniffling, twitching etc. It is bewildering to watch his shifting moods or listen to his never-ending complaints and arguments. Suddenly, nothing suits his taste. Life becomes a series of daily irritations.

The adolescents are full of contradictions. He fights getting up in the morning, and he fights going to bed at night. He is behind in his studies and in sports. His language is rude, but he is too shy at the same time. He will quarrel and quibble and ignore our words. He will be critical of us. But he will be genuinely surprised if we feel hurt.

We can be consoled because his behaviour fits his developmental phase. The purpose of adolescence is to loosen personality. His personality is undergoing the required changes. From organization (the childhood) through disorganization (Adolescence) to reorganization (Adulthood). Adolescence is a period of curative madness, in which every teenager has to remake his personality. He has to free himself from childhood ties with parents, establish new identifications with peers, and find his own identity.

ADOLESCENTS

Introduction

The word 'Adolescence' comes from the Latin verb 'Adolescere' which means 'to grow'. So the essence of the word adolescence is growth and it is in this sense that adolescence represents a period of intensive growth and change in nearly all aspects of child's physical, mental, social, emotional, religious and moral life. It is a very crucial period of one's life.

Who is an Adolescent?

A child is described as an adolescent when he or she reaches puberty, that is when he has become sexually mature to the point, where he is able to reproduce his kind. He ceases to be an adolescent when he has acquired maturity to play the role of an adult in his society or culture. Maturity, as the term used here, does not mean mere physical maturity, it also implies mental, emotional and social maturity.

Fig. 12. 3. Adolescent boys and girl

It is very difficult to point out the exact range of the adolescence period in terms of chronological years. Achieving puberty and becoming mature cannot be tied to a universal span or period. In our country in comparison to western countries, the period of adolescence starts early as Indian children achieve puberty earlier, due to the favourable climatic and cultural factors. Also it ends earlier due to easy attainment of maturity whereas in the western world "the adolescence extends roughly from 13 years of age till 21 for girls and 15 till 21 for boys", In India it usually ranges from 13 to 19 among boys and from 11 to 17 among girls. Yet there are wide individual differences. To quote a IVth standard teacher, she was so surprised to see that few of her girls in her class had already reached puberty. Some girls achieve puberty these days between 9 and 10 years of age. Therefore, the range of adolescence, not only differs from country to country but varies from community to community and from individual to individual. In general, girls become sexually as well as socially mature at an early age. The standard of living, diet, early or late marriage, health and climate, the cultural traditions and environment, attitude towards other sex and the role expected from the child at different ages are some of the other factors which control the dawn of puberty and attainment of maturity by children.

The above classifications of the range for the period of adolescence are not rigid as explained above. There are wide individual differences. However with a view of a rough estimate for universal applicability, with regard to span of adolescence the adolescents can be referred to as teenagers — the individuals having chronological age between 11 to 19 years.

CHARACTERISTICS OF ADOLESCENTS

The human growth and development takes a spiral form and not linear. Therefore, within the alternate stages of life, we find a sort of repetition and resemblance of characteristics. The old adults are often found to behave like children. In adolescence also we find a sort of repetition and recapitulation of what has been done during infancy. Thus Ross says, "Adolescence is best regarded as a recapitulation of the first period of life, as second turn of the spiral of development". Like infancy, the adolescence is the period of too much restlessness and disturbances. To quote Stanley Hall, "It is a period of great stress and strain, storm and strife".

The adolescents' growth and developmental pattern along with the peculiar characteristics of this age can help us in understanding our adolescents.

The challenge of parenting teenagers is two-fold. They are changing dramatically and we are often unprepared for how their changing behaviour will affect us. The relationship between parent and child involves a delicate balance between our personality type and our child's. Developmentally, teenagers are changing dramatically in seven ways: physically, intellectually, emotionally, sexually, socially, spiritually and morally. These developmental behaviours are temporary and universal. These behaviours are particularly characteristic of the early teenage years, from eleven to fifteen years.

PHYSICAL DEVELOPMENT AND CHANGES

During this stage, the physical growth and development reaches its peak and boys and girls get their final body shape. The maximum increase in size, weight and height is achieved. The average girl reaches her mature height between the ages of 17 and 18 and an average boy, a year or so later. Bones and muscles increase to the greatest possible extent leading to increased motor activity. The various parts of the body gradually come into proportion. The trunk of the body broadens and lengthens, and thus the limbs no longer seem too long.

Fig. 12.4. Physical development in adolescents

The growth and function of all other outer and inner organs also reaches to its maximum and almost all the glands become extremely active at this age. Both male and female sex organs reach their mature size in late adolescence. Boys and girls develop the characteristic features of their respective sexes. There is the roundness of the breasts and hips among girls and growth of facial hair for boys. There is a distinct change in voice among the two sexes. While the girls voice acquire shrillness and become sweet, the boys voice deepen and becomes harsher. The girls begin to menstruate monthly during this period and the boys have nocturnal emissions accompanied by erotic dreams. These biological changes trigger an increased interest in body's image.

INTELLECTUAL DEVELOPMENT

This is the period when adolescents begin to think operationally. Intelligence reaches its climax during this period. Intellectual powers like logical thinking, abstract reasoning and concentration are almost developed up to the end of this period. An adolescent learns to reason and seeks answer to 'how and why' of everything scientifically. His power of critical thinking and observation are

Fig. 12.5. Sharing scientific concepts with the great scientist- Dr. A.P.J. Abdul Kalam, ex-President of India.

developed. He is critical of almost everything. He develops fine imagination. Writers, artists, poets, philosophers, and inventors are all born in this period. Improper channelization of imagination and dissatisfied needs may turn an adolescent into day-dreaming. Therefore great care has to be taken for cultivating their power of imagination.

EMOTIONAL DEVELOPMENT

A teenager's emotional development is influenced by biological, cognitive and social factors. As parents and educators, we need to recognize the impact that our society has on our own children.

Emotional development reaches its maximum during adolescence. It is a time of heightened emotional tension resulting from the physical and glandular changes that are taking place. It is a period of heightening of all emotions like anxiety, fear, love and anger. Just like during the infancy, the individual experiences emotional instability and intensity during adolescence. He is too touchy, sensitive, inflammable and moody.

Ross says, "The adolescent lives an intensely emotional life in which we can see once more the rhythm of positive and negative phases of behaviour in his constant alternation between intense excitement and 'deep depression". This is why

Fig. 12.6. Emotional expressions of adolescents

the period is often designated as a period of stresses and strains. Their emotions fluctuate very frequently.

It is very difficult to put a check on the emotions during the peak of adolescence. In fact during adolescence emotions take their roots into sentiments. Self-consciousness, self-respect and personal pride is increased much more. Group loyalty and sentiments of love are developed which make an adolescent sentimental and passionate. What he feels, he feels it very strongly and when he reacts, he reacts vigorously. There is an increased desire to be alone and a tendency to exaggerate.

SOCIAL DEVELOPMENT

Fig. 12.7. Adolescents' clique

Adolescents spend more time with their peers. Friends become increasingly more important, acceptance by peers is a strong motivation for most teenagers. An adolescent develops a good amount of social sense as compared to a child who cares very little for the society. An adolescent is no more ego-centric or selfish. He is more social. He wants to mould his behaviour according to the norms of the society.

The social circle of an adolescent is very wide. He becomes interested in opposite sex. He believes in making intimate friendship and attaches himself closely to a group. The adolescent usually has two or three close friends, or confidants. They are of the same sex and have similar interests and abilities. Close friends have a marked influence on another, though they may quarrel occasionally.

Cliques are usually made up of close friends. At first they consist of members of the same sex, but later include both boys and girls.

Crowds, made up of cliques and groups of close friends develop interest in parties and dating grows.

Organized groups are established by schools and community organizations to meet the social needs of adolescents who belong to no cliques or crowds.

An adolescent believes in making intimate friendship and attaches himself closely to a group. Peer group relationship controls the social behaviour of this age. The child develops a strong sense of loyalty towards the group. He wants to be accepted by the group of which he is a member. The rejection is costly.

The adolescent craves for independence. He wants that his personality should be recognized by the parents and elderly members of the family. He doesn't want to be treated as a child. He gives more importance to the values and beliefs maintained by his peer group than the advice of his parents. There may even be hidden or open rebellion if the parents try to impose their opinion.

Girls can hate other girls who do not conform to the culture's idea of feminity. Some smart and assertive girls are likely to be criticized by other girls while boys who are cool and strong may criticize the boys who are sensitive and open.

Adolescents do not want their parents to enquire about their boy friends or girl friends. They have quite a bit of knowledge about sex and sexuality, though much of their information is incomplete and inaccurate.

Adolescents enjoy travelling during vacations and far away places, away from home. They enjoy relaxing and talking with their friends. They enjoy reading, music and dance. Going to the movies is a favourite clique activity.

Fig. 12.8. A very close adolescent girls' pair

Day dreaming and hero/heroine worshipping are popular recreation among all adolescents when they are bored or lonely.

Every adolescent sooner or later discovers that money is the key to independence. Interest in money therefore becomes an important element in independence. This interest centres mainly on how to earn more money, regardless of the kind of work done.

SEXUAL DEVELOPMENT

Sexual development reaches its peak during adolescence. The adolescent is sexually mature. During adolescence the sexual development like infancy goes into three stages as :

1. **Stage of Auto-erotism or Self-love :** At this stage the young boys and girls fall in love with themselves. They try to take pleasure with their own bodies. Self-decoration and enjoying it before the mirror is their common practice. Self-enjoyment by indulging in masturbation is also prevalent at this stage.

2. **Stage of Homo-Sexuality :** At this stage boys and girls are attracted towards the members of their own sex and seek gratification from each other's body by grouping them in two or three at one time.

Fig. 12.9.   Self-decoration

Fig. 12.10.   A close adolescent boys' pair

Fig. 12.11. Hetero-sexual friendship

3. Hetero-Sexual Stage : At this stage boys and girls are seen attracted towards each other. They are keen to make friendship or establish even sexual relationship with the members of the opposite sex.

Due to their growing interest in sex, adolescent boys and girls seek more and more information about it. Few adolescents feel that they can learn all they want to know about sex from their parents. Consequently, they take advantage of whatever sources of information that are available to them.

Studies of what adolescents are primarily interested in knowing about sex have revealed that girls are especially curious about birth control, the "Pill" abortion and pregnancy. Boys, on the other hand, want to know about venereal diseases, enjoyment of sex and birth control.

In our permissive modern society, the

Fig. 12.12. Encouraging respect for life and abstinence

adolescents need a good guidance programme on sex and sexuality. The need for sex education is a must in the schools and colleges.

SPIRITUAL AND MORAL DEVELOPMENT

Adolescents of today are interested in religion and feel that it plays an important role in their lives. They talk about God, religion and religious values. Adolescents are drawn towards a deeper spirituality than when they were children. It is during this time that the individuals begin to take personal responsibility for their religious beliefs. Some become deeply religious, others experience a crises in faith, while others may not believe in any particular religion. Many boys and girls begin to question the religious concepts and beliefs of their childhood and this has led adolescence to question religion. Many adolescents investigate their religion as a source of emotional and intellectual stimulation. Due to their increased ability to think abstractly, adolescents are more interested in religious and spiritual matters. They do wonder about the ultimate life. They question about; life, death, life after death etc. They do believe in a Supreme Being (God).

Fig. 12.13. Adolescents respect prayer and God

With the development of social and civic sense, the children during this period learn to behave according to the norms of their society and culture. Also the group sense makes them follow some moral or ethical code. The formation of strong sentiments during this period intensifies the process of moral development.

SPECIAL FEATURES AND NEEDS OF ADOLESCENTS

Somatic variations and secondary sex characteristics

The adolescents have a more or less difficult task of adjusting to the changes in body and to the secondary sex characteristics due to the sudden functioning of their glands and the secretion of sex hormones.

The adolescent, with his nearly developed body, is constantly making comparisons between himself and his contemporaries. Differences are almost certain to cause him some anxiety. They are particularly concerned with height, weight, fatness, thinness, facial blemishes, width of the hips and breasts size in girls and of the genitals in boys. In some cases boys become very self-conscious due to the deepening and harshness of voice. Girls want to look feminine and attractive to boys. Boys want to look manly to gain prestige among other boys and particularly among girls. Any deviation from the norms and standard of the peer group can produce complexes in the mind and make him maladjusted.

Fig. 12.14. Weight gain in an adolescent boy

Fig. 12.15. Rapid physical growth in girls

Rapid growth and body changes are likely to be accompanied by fatigue, listlessness and other unfavourable symptoms. Digestive disturbances are frequent and appetite is finicky. The glandular changes and the changes in the size and position of the internal organs upsets the adolescents. These changes interfere with the normal functions of digestion. Anemia is common at this period, not because of marked changes in blood chemistry, but because of erratic eating habits, which in turn increase the already present tendency to be tired and listless.

The flow of blood during menstruation creates worries among the girls and gives birth to so many fears and anxieties. Similarly, the discharge of the semen during nocturnal emission among boys horrifies them. During the early menstrual periods, girls frequently experience headaches, backaches, cramps, and abdominal pain, accompanied by fainting, vomiting, skin irritations and even swelling of the legs and ankles. As a result they feel tired, depressed, and irritable at the time of their periods. As menstruation becomes more regular, the physical and psychological disturbances which accompany its early appearances tend to diminish.

Fig. 12.16. An understanding friend

Fig. 12.17. A mother is trying to convince/console her daughter

Headaches, backaches and a general feeling of acheness occurs at other times between menstruation. Both boys and girls suffer intermittently from these discomforts, their frequency and severity depending to a large extent upon how rapidly the pubescent changes are occurring and upon how healthy the individuals are when puberty began.

Puberty may be regarded as a sickly age and if pubescent children are actually ill, they need to be treated with more sympathy and understanding, and their unsocial behaviour needs to be tolerated.

Adolescents become too Self-conscious

There is a strong desire in an adolescent that his or her bodily changes should be noticed by the elders and by peer group. Boys and girls pay more attention towards their dresses, make-up, manner of talking, walking, eating etc.

They crave for recognition and they want to be the centre of attraction for the opposite sex. They want their abilities, intelligence and capacities to be recognized by the peer group and elders. They are too much sensitive, touchy and inflammable. They aim to maintain their concept of themselves and their status among their peers at any cost. Any attack on their phenomenal self will be reacted and with behavioural problems like aggressiveness or with withdrawal symptoms.

Sex consciousness becomes too intense at this time. Most of their problems are concerned with the sudden functioning of their glands, secretion of sex hormones and the awakening of the strong sex instinct. (see Sexual development.)

Independence v/s Dependence :

"Don't treat me like a child", Almost all the adolescents react strongly with this statement to their parents at one time or the other. The adolescent wants to be totally independent and he asserts himself to show that he is a mature person.

On the other hand, he is typically a person who needs security, guidance and protection like a child. His abilities and capacities are still in the process of growth and development. He depends on his parents and elders for the satisfaction of his many needs like physical, emotional and economic. His intense love for thrill and adventure coupled with his uncontrolled emotions needs somebody to guide him and to check his unbridled flow of energy.

Peer Group Relationship: The adolescent spends much of his time with the members of his peer group as discussed earlier. He follows the ideals of the group. He wants to be fully accepted by his peers. Nothing can be more devastating to the adolescent than to be rejected by his age-mates.

Idealism v/s Realism: The adolescent desires to help in the creation of an ideal society. He is very critical of the existing circumstances and happenings. He questions about inequality, injustice, corruption and sufferings. He wants to reform the world.

In his search of idealism he goes away from realism. He tends to accept the impossible. When it is not attainable he becomes quite disturbed and unreasonable. He turns himself into a problem youth. Such adolescents withdraw into their own world, they become anti-social and maladjusted persons.

VOCATIONAL CHOICE AND NEED OF SELF-SUPPORT

The adolescent's strong desire is to achieve self-sufficiency and make himself quite independent. Preparing for the future career is essential at this time. Vocational choice is an important one for the adolescent and he finds himself not quite up to the mark in making a right choice. Therefore, the adolescents want proper guidance and advice with regard to their interests, aptitudes and vocational choices.

Need to Belong to a Peer Group : Socially he has a strong need to belong to a peer group. On the other hand, emotionally he needs to be loved, accepted and admired. He needs security, freedom from anxiety and recognition of self. There is a striving need for independence from parental control and a struggle for making the active sexual instincts and urges sublimated within the norms of the society and culture.

All these demand proper direction and guidance to the adolescents from parents, teachers, guidance workers and career counsellors. The educational process, the parental care, the efforts of the teachers and the environmental conditions should be designed to ensure proper growth and development of the adolescents and channelizations of their energies in a proper direction.

What do adolescent boys worry about? (13 Years to 16 years old.)

Family

Parents, their relationship with parents, stable family, family finance, crisis in family, divorce, separation, getting parents permission for activities, getting money from parents.

School

Achievement in school, passing, getting through school, doing well in school, winning the game, making the team, vocational choice, general achievement, acceptance by others, acceptance by girls, acceptance by peer group, parental acceptance and approval.

Money

Money for dates, for personal use, for future.

Personal Characteristics

Being grown up so quickly, self-conscious, awkward, physical characteristics, weakness, appearance, guilt feelings, guilty conscience.

What do adolescent females worry about? (11 Years to 16 years old.)

Family

Parents, their relationship with parents, stable family, family finance, crisis in family, divorce, separation, health of the parents, future of brothers and sisters, independence, obligation to the family, mother.

School

Grades, doing well in exams, meeting deadlines, doing assignments, work on time, school work, studies in general, getting through school, scholarship.

Social relationship

Being accepted by peer group, being liked, what others think, feeling shy, inferiority complex. Boyfriends, meaningful relationship with them, fear of hurting others.

Money

For personal use, for social get-together, money for future.

Future in general

Stable, happy, secure future.

Marriage

Getting married, meeting the right man I can love, and love me, future family happiness. Being a good wife.

Sex

Abstaining from pre-marital sex, mother finding out that her daughter is taking birth control pills, sex obligation in future, overweight.

TEENAGERS' EXPECTATIONS FROM THEIR PARENTS AND ELDERS

❖ They need unconditional love.

❖ They expect respect and they want to be taken seriously.

❖ They need to be treated as adults and equals, "Don't treat me like a child".

❖ They need affection, acceptance, approval, achievement and affirmation.

❖ They expect privacy and freedom.

❖ They need space.

❖ They need a listening heart rather than just the ears.

❖ They expect equality and justice in everything.

❖ They expect short and straight forward answers rather than lengthy instructions.

❖ They want consistency.

❖ They want their parents to be direct instead of beating around the bush.

❖ They expect trust, openness and honesty in word and action.

❖ Each adolescent expects his parents to accept him as a unique individual.

❖ They want their plans to be honoured and respected.

❖ They want to take some responsibility in the family.

❖ They appreciate democratic style of parenting.

❖ They want to be a part of the family discussions.

❖ They like to organize family outings and fun.

❖ They want to keep the budget.

❖ They want their friends to join family meals at times.

❖ They expect their parents "to admit their mistakes".

❖ They prefer reconciliation and forgiveness.

❖ They want the past faults to be forgotten and Let Go of the Past!

❖ They expect their parents to have disagreement and arguments. But they NEVER WANT THEIR PARENTS TO FIGHT, TO SEPARATE OR DIVORCE. THEY WANT THEIR PARENTS LIVING TOGETHER AS ADULTS.

SOME PROBLEMS AND BEHAVIOURAL DISORDERS OF ADOLESCENTS

Most of the problems of adolescents are concerned with the sudden functioning of their glands and secretion of hormones. In some cases, certain unfavourable factors in the environment are responsible.

❖ Too self-conscious

❖ Loss of self-confidence

❖ Too curious about sex./Pre-marital sex./ Experimenting with sex.

❖ Boredom

❖ Isolation or withdrawal syndrome.

❖ Social Antagonism, Rebellion.

❖ Moodiness - fluctuating moods

❖ Temper tantrums

❖ Irritability

❖ Too touchy

❖ Stuttering/stammering

❖ Nail-biting

❖ Nose-pricking

❖ Finger-drumming

❖ Feet-tapping, throat clearing, squinting.

❖ Sniffling, twitching or grimacing

❖ Excessive day-dreaming

❖ Regression

❖ Excessive use of defense mechanisms such as rationalization, projection, fantasising, compensation, identification and displacement.

❖ Anti-social activities

❖ Reckless driving

❖ Excessive drinking

❖ Use of drugs

❖ Smoking

❖ Depression

TEENAGE DRIVING

There are sixteen-year-old who handle a car with skill and confidence; they drive better than their parents, while some eighteen-year-old may be reckless drivers or immature and irresponsible in handling the wheel.

Fig. 12.18. Teenage driving

All parents want their teenagers to become experienced and responsible drivers. They cannot do so without our help. Parents need to offer opportunities for responsible driving, while simultaneously setting clear limits and sensible regulations. A car has a unique symbolic value to the teenagers. It is an emblem of adulthood. It represents freedom and power, speed and excitement. Therefore, it can be dangerous in the hands of the immature adolescents.

Some guidelines given by parents will be of great help.

● Every teenager should have the opportunity to take driving education courses.

● A minimum six months of driving with a restricted license should precede the obtainment of an unrestricted license by teenagers.

● The minimum age for car ownership should be 18.

● No teenager should own a car unless he can pay for it and maintain it out of his own earnings. Even in affluent homes responsibility is demanded for the privilege provided.

● Traffic laws must be obeyed. Traffic misdemeanour is as dangerous as a felony. When life is at stake, there can be no second and third chances.

- Teenage drivers should be clearly aware of their legal and financial responsibilities.

TEENAGE DRINKING

Apart from legal and social standards, many parents have strong personal feelings about alcohol.

Why Do Teenagers Drink?

For a teenager alcohol is a symbol of maturity. He drinks to stimulate sophistication and to defy authority. It is a proclamation of adulthood. The more rebellious a teenager is, the earlier he will pursue alcohol and other pleasures reserved for adults since resentment of authority motivates drinking. There are no

Fig. 12.19. Teenage drinking

quick antidotes. Alcohol is readily available, relatively inexpensive and seemingly safe. It brings pleasure and confers status on them. To persuade teenagers to abstain from alcohol is not a simple matter.

Prevention and Guidelines to Drinking

Research indicates that many problem drinkers show distinct personality traits. They are impulsive, they overemphasise masculinity and tend to deny their anxiety and dependency. Prevention of problem drinking can take two directions. One is to strengthen the personality and character of our youth. The second is to divest alcohol of its status.

Parents need to help the teenagers in learning to live with his drinking or non-drinking. It takes courage to say "no, thanks" when drinks are offered at a party. One needs to learn to say it without an apology, explanation, argument or excuse. One father told his nineteen-year-old son, "Assume that your no thanks will be respected. Say it firmly. Don't explain and don't complain."

DRUGS ABUSE

Fig. 12.20. Teenage and drugs

Millions of young people have experimented with drugs that affect mind and mood. Many try them once or twice and quit. Others continue and get "hooked." Some teenagers use drugs for kicks. To get high, they are willing to try almost anything. They are blind to dangers and deaf to warnings.

The tide of addiction can be turned back only through prevention.

TEENAGE SMOKING

For a teenager, smoking is again a symbol of maturity and sophistication just like alcohol. Teenagers resort to smoking to deny their anxiety.

Those teenagers who drink, smoke or take drugs show distinct personality traits. They are impulsive and tend to deny their anxiety.

The best way to help them would be to strengthen their personality and character. Engage them in worthwhile activities both physically and mentally.

Fig. 12.21. Teenage smoking

TEENAGE   DEPRESSION

Fig. 12.22. Depressed teenagers

Come, March, April, May, we keep hearing and reading in the Newspapers about teenage boys and girls committing suicide or running away from home after the Xth, XIIth standard exams. The trend of committing suicide has started after the CET exams and before admission to the professional courses.

Student ends life

A student of BMS College of Women committed suicide at her house in Nagendra Block in Hanumanthanagar on Friday. Academic failure is said to be the reason. The deceased has been identified as a final year B.Com student. According to the police, she was disappointed with her performance in the examination.

Courtesy: The Times of India, Bangalore.

SSLC student commits suicide

TIMES NEWS NETWORK

Domlur : Faced with the fear of not being able to fare well in an examination, a 16 - year-old boy committed suicide on Monday night in his house in Domlur Layout,

The boy, a student of BHS School, was to write his maths examination of Tuesday.

In another case Betty (name changed) a IX standard girl, was taken to the ICU of a hospital after she was found unconscious in her bedroom. She swallowed more than 55 tablets of various kinds which were her parents' medicines. Why? She was depressed and wanted to die.

She made another attempt to commit suicide and ended up again in the hospital. But she was lucky to have caring parents and they sought professional help for her. After a couple of years of therapy and antidepressants, she came back to her normal self. She achieved a wonderful XII standard result and joined her brother in USA for higher studies, making her parents and herself proud. What was the reason for her depression? A younger brother was born in the family after a gap of 12 years. She found it difficult to accept the younger sibling and resented the love her parents shared with the younger one.

Jatin, a 15-year-old, was on the verge of committing suicide when his wise and sensitive grandfather (who is a doctor) observed his low moods and other problematic behaviour. He was given immediate help. The main reason for his depression was that his parents were engaged in a legal battle for divorce.

Parental pressures and rising academic expectations pushed Meena almost over the edge. This is what she expressed in a letter after she got her first term report card.

> I am not satisfied with my result.
> I don't want to go home. I don't want to show my result to my family members, because they won't appreciate it. I don't even want to talk to my elder brother on phone who is going to call up tomorrow. He will be very depressed to and unhappy to on knowing about my result to Today I don't like anything I see. Even the most beautiful and precious thing seems to be worthless. I don't want to be study anymore, and continue to be a source of trouble for my parents.
>
> English – 80 (85)
> Hindi – 72 (80)
> Maths – 90 (90)
> S. Studies – 85 (90)
> Science – 90 (95)

Thanks are due to her class teacher and the school for helping her to come out of the depression and helping her parents to have a realistic attitude towards their daughter.

In the 21st century, the onset of depression in children and adolescence is increasingly common. A decade ago, doctors considered depression to be strictly an adult disease. Teenage irritability, mood fluctuation and rebelliousness were considered "just a passing phase" which children would outgrow. Now researchers believe that if this behaviour is chronic, it may signal serious problems. Early untreated depression can also increase chances of more severe depression and personality disorders in later life.

SOME CAUSES OF DEPRESSION IN TEENAGERS

STRESS IN THE FAMILY

* Parental neglect, constant friction between parents and the growing rate of divorce.
* Parental pressures and the unrealistic academic expectations of teenagers themselves.
* Social pressures
* Child abuse
* Hormonal surges of puberty and changes in brain structure
* Genetic cause - if either parent had depression
* Drugs or alcohol addicted parents
* Poor vocational preparation and inappropriate vocational choice.

SYMPTOMS OF DEPRESSION IN TEENS

* Excessive moodiness, sadness and irritability
* Negativism
* Low self-esteem
* Feeling of helplessness and worthlessness
* Lethargy
* In some cases insomnia and in other cases continuous sleeping
* Too much clinging to someone for security
* Lack of interest in play, reading or in any other recreational activities
* Withdrawal
* Anti-social behaviours like lying, cheating, playing truant and stealing etc.
* Nightmares
* School phobia
* Depressed adolescents may start smoking and drinking. They are at high risk for school failure, social isolation, promiscuity, self-medication with drugs and even suicide.

TREATMENT OF TEENAGE DEPRESSION

Most cases of childhood depression can be successfully treated if detected early. Both antidepressant medications and cognitive behavioural therapy have helped many depressed teens to come back to normal life.

Research on the use of drugs for treating depression is still going on along with behavioural therapy.

Depressed adolescents are more changeable and reactive to the environment than depressed adults. If a teenager goes for a picnic, he may enjoy himself but once he is back at home he is likely to be depressed again. While a depressed adult may never make it for a picnic or even if he goes, he may be a depressed man during the picnic.

If detected early, most of the depressed adolescents can be treated with medicine and counselling or by changing the environment. If you suspect that your child is depressed, seek professional help immediately. Don't ever neglect a child's strange behaviour as unimportant. Children's feelings also need to be respected just as much as that of adults.

However, prevention of depression in children is better than treatment. Both the parents and the teachers can help in the prevention of depression in children.

GUIDANCE AND COUNSELLING FOR ADOLESCENTS

After having a look into the adolescents' characteristics, needs and expectations and their problems and behavioural disorders, we realize that many of them need a good guidance and counselling programme in order to make proper adjustment in life. If they are not given the guidance programme at the right time they will be maladjusted in the society.

Recent researches in the field of adolescents' psychology have revealed that the adults, the parents, the teachers and their unreasonable ways and views are the real problems of adolescence. They forget that there is a gap between them and the adolescents. In dealing with them, the parents and the teacher should realize that the demands of their peer group are more important than their own expectations.

In the adolescents there is a need for respect and recognition and they also maintain their self-prestige and status among their peers.

The adolescents' five needs; affection, acceptance, approval, achievement and self-actualization must be met. If these needs are not met, there will be unhappiness, and insecurity in them and can cause maladjustment in their lives.

Besides these, the members of the family and teachers need to be gentle yet firm and understand their physical, mental and emotional changes.

Fig. 12.23. Father and son

Due to the sudden physical changes, the adolescents can become too self-conscious, as a result they lose self-confidence. This may result in fear, anxiety and nervousness.

Neeraj, 15-year-old was a well-built, tall and handsome boy but used to stutter in front of his teachers, elders or in front of any authority. Never had he any stuttering when he was in VIth or VIIth standard. While counselling it was found out that his problem of stuttering started after he had a bad experience with his father and the father ridiculed him for his way of talking. This made him quite frightened as well as humiliated.

While in another case, an VIIIth standard boy all of a sudden started keeping quiet in the class and later when he was coaxed to speak, he was stammering and he had totally lost his fluency in speaking. When traced back, it revealed that he was teased by his own classmates, both girls and boys due to the sudden change in his voice.

In both the cases, their disorders were corrected easily and in time due to the timely and appropriate guidance programmes. The above type of behaviour disorders may not happen in every case, but in some cases it does happen and they are corrected and in some cases they are not helped to correct it. As a result, we do come across some grown-up individuals still stuttering or stammering.

Girls need guidance to adjust with the discomfort and irritability of menstrual periods. Many girls become very moody, touchy and show temper tantrums just before and during the menstrual periods. Once a father said, "My daughter has become so cranky due to her physical changes, so I've put her in a hostel". In some severe cases, fainting and vomiting are also common. These girls, need a better understanding of the menstrual periods and they need to develop a positive attitude towards it. So that they will accept and appreciate the purpose of having the menstrual period and it will help them from having the fainting spells, vomiting and other severe pains associated with it. In case there is any physical cause for such problems, it has to be treated medically.

Teenagers are eager to learn all they can about sex. They are bothered and perplexed and want realistic and personal answers. Sex is already being "taught" - on the screen, in the school, and in the streets. In words and pictures, our children are exposed to sex that is often sordid and vulgar. Our streets are a ceaseless source of misinformation. **IT IS THE PARENTS AND TEACHERS WHO OFTEN FEAR TO SHARE INTIMATE INFORMATION WITH THE TEENAGE BOYS AND GIRLS.**

MEENAKSHI NAYAR Sex Educator, New Delhi

"When we approach them with our workshop, the common excuse in schools is parents will object. But 90% of parents say yes to it."

R. KISHORE KUMAR Senior principal, St. John's International Residential School, Chennai

"A residential school has bigger responsibilities than a day-school. Sex education should be dealt with from Class IX."

MANISHA MALHOTRA Trainer, Shri Ram School, New Delhi

"They are like the moral police—teachers are so inhibited that they are embarrassed to teach even routine biology lessons."

Courtesy : | OUTLOOK | 11 OCTOBER 2004

Veena, 17-year-old says, "My mother believes that ignorance assures innocence, she gets mad when I ask her anything about sex. She says, "Your husband will teach you all that what you have to know."

Sex sensation combined with curiosity about sex draws members of the two opposite sex nearer and nearer. This may result in pre-marital sex and intercourse. These activities create so many worries and complexities and guilt feelings in the adolescents. It can also ruin their future lives.

Certain gynaecologists in the cities get calls almost everyday from the college going girls for abortion. It is common among the hostel girls. Teenage pregnancies and HIV infections are quite alarming in many cities.

This is an area where the adolescents need proper guidance. Both the parents and teachers share the responsibility to be frank and honest with the adolescents about sex.

It is a girl's task not to allow herself to be used as a tool. It is a boy's obligation not to use a girl as an object. Both boys and girls need to know that not all is fair in love and sex. It is unfair for a girl to tease and provoke a boy. It is unfair for a boy to place the whole burden of decisions on the girls. In the old pattern, a boy tried to go as far as the girl would let him, without questioning her readiness or his responsibility. Young people need to be taught to face such issues honestly. Open discussions about mutual responsibility can enhance our teenagers' capacity to make wise decisions about love and life.

Sex is more of a problem to teenagers than to any other group. Their desire is easily triggered. Their passion is at a peak. Sources of arousal are plentiful, but sexual intercourse is prohibited. Hence, masturbation is a common outlet.

Masturbation is self-stimulation of the genital organs to achieve sexual satisfaction. Though it may release physical tensions, it does not satisfy the spirit. It does not fulfill the yearning for intimacy, for love, for affirmation. Masturbation is so self-centered. Instead of intense intimacy there is spurious autonomy. According to a medical journal of 1885, masturbation causes cancer, heart disease, hysteria, convulsions, impotence, frigidity and insanity. Today, we know that masturbation does not even cause pimples, let alone disastrous diseases. Many boys develop psychological problems due to several misgivings about masturbation. It is still a source of anxiety to many teenagers. To escape it, they may resort to pre-marital sex. Pre-marital sex is wrong so is the practice of masturbation. Discipline and self-control can prevent masturbation and pre-marital sex.

Day-dreaming is another common outlet for the teenagers. Masturbation and day-dreaming are helpful as a temporary escape from tension and other frustrations. But they can become an easy substitute for effort and for disappointment and defeat. They want to come to terms with their sexuality and to integrate it into their total personality.

Therefore **Sex Education** for teenagers is one of the best educational programmes for their wholesome development. Sex education has two parts-Information and Values.

Teamwork

When geese fly in formation,
they travel about 70% faster than
when they fly alone.

Geese share leadership. When the
lead goose tires, he (or she) rotates back
into the "V" and another flies forward
to become the leader.

Geese keep company with the fallen. When
a sick or weak goose drops out of flight
formation, at least one other goose joins to help
and protect.

By being part of a team, we too, can accomplish
much more, much faster. Words of encouragement
and support (honking from behind) help inspire and
energize those on the front line, helping them to keep
pace in spite of the day-to-day pressures and fatigue.

And, finally, show compassion and care for our fellow
men - a member of the ultimate team; "mankind".

The next time you see a formation of geese, remember that it
is a reward, a challenge, and a privilege to be a contributing
member of a team.

Values are best learned at home and school. Information can at best be given by experts. In the school curriculum for the teenagers, there should be a period provided for sex education. Many of the information can be given by experts only. Some parents need protection against harassment. Disguised as a quest for enlightenment, not all questions on sex spring from a thirst for knowledge. Some aim to vex and embarrass. Parents need not answer provocative questions. They are entitled to their modesty, discomfort, and lack of specific information. What about information sought genuinely? Again, within the limits of knowledge and comfort, answers should be provided. Other questions are best referred to experts. Parents should encourage their teenagers to take part in discussions on sex sponsored by the school, college, church, and other community centres. Information imparted with objectivity and honesty may decrease hostility and increase trust between the generations. Adults may regain their faith in youth. The young people may find that despite the age gap, adults share with them a common knowledge.

Alongwith proper guidance, the teenagers need to be fully occupied physically and mentally.

Fig. 12.24. Running race

Fig. 12.25. Tug of war

Fig. 12.26. Swimming

During adolescence, bones and muscles increase to the greatest possible extent leading to a great increase in motor activity. The schools and colleges should provide enough activities, which would give them a channel to release all their pent up energy. For example, for boys such vigorous games like football, basketball, baseball, swimming, cricket and other field and track events give lots of physical exercises. Adolescents like adventure and fun like mountaineering, trekking, rock climbing etc. Besides these, work experience projects, social service projects are introduced like scouting, N.C.C., R.S.P., Sea-cadets, and so on. The adolescents association and such bodies will help the individual to

Fig. 12.27. N.C.C. students

develop his abilities to the fullest. These activities not only help the individual to be fully occupied, but they help in the development of several social and moral values like, cooperation, team-spirit, self-sacrifice, forgiveness and sportsmanship.

The above activities will help the adolescents emotionally and sexually. All the pent up emotions, physical and sexual energies will be released and the adolescents will become more calm and disciplined instead of daydreaming about other useless activities.

Girls also could be occupied with certain physical activities like sports/tennis, throwball, basketball, scouting and guiding etc. Physical exercises are good for their physical fitness.

Fig. 12.28. Skipping

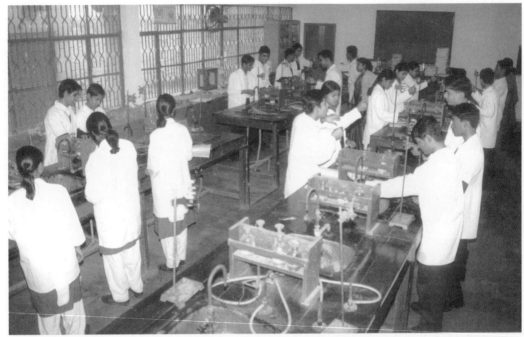

Fig. 12.29. Students in science lab

Fig. 12.30. Students paying their tribute to Mahatma Gandhi at Raj Ghat, New Delhi

Both boys and girls should be provided with physically and mentally stimulating activities in the school. The more challenging the activities, the better it is for the students. Activities like projects, group discussions, group teaching, quiz programmes, drama, music, essay competitions, field trips, excursions etc. will stimulate them mentally. Socially and morally, they will develop many virtues for group and community living as mentioned above.

If both the boys and girls are physically and mentally occupied, some of the behavioural disorders like boredom, depressive tendencies, irritability, nail-biting, finger drumming, day-dreaming and anti-social activities can be prevented.

November-Monday

November-Tuesday

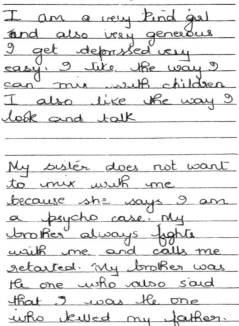

I am a very kind girl and also very generous. I get depressed very easy. I like the way I can mix with children I also like the way I look and talk

My sister does not want to mix with me because she says I am a psycho case. My brother always fights with me and calls me retarted. My brother was the one who also said that I was the one who killed my father.

I do like all of them in my house. But I don't think any one seems to care about me.

I had to give away four of my pet dogs because the neighbours were hurting them. It was very sad because everything I love I had to loose. When my sister goes out for any dance and I can't go because I don't have anyone to take me out as I am not as beautiful as my sister.

Thus, vigorous physical and mental exercises will help the adolescents to glide into maturity and help them to become a well-balanced person.

EDUCATIONAL GUIDANCE FOR ADOLESCENTS

Adolescents demand independence. Hence the teacher must provide possible opportunities for self-study and self-expression. The teacher would do well to allow the students to participate in the planning of the class and school activities. These youngsters are also mature enough to shoulder responsibilities. Moreover educators have noticed that rules and regulations framed with the assistance of the students can be easily enforced and they are readily obeyed. It is also noticed that they themselves come up with certain disciplinary actions for them. It works wonders and the administration is on an advantageous position in this regard. This type of democratic functioning with the student bodies helps them to be better quality leaders in the future.

Teachers must be patient and tactful in all their dealings with the adolescents. They should guard against hurting the feelings or unnecessarily challenging these young people. We must remember that youth gangs are very headstrong. Though they can do excellent constructive work, provocative situations can arouse very destructive tendencies in them. Simplicity, sincerity and a friendly attitude however works wonders with these young people. The teacher must make the adolescent feel that he / she is really interested in them. Once they spot a friendly adult who is ready to understand them, they become the nicest people on earth.

Adolescents will not tolerate from teachers, favouritism, inequalities, injustice and double standards. They easily locate the double standards adopted by the teachers and then the gap between the two goes on widening as discussed earlier. The adolescents have attained full mental functioning. Therefore abstract reasoning and concentration is developed. The adolescent learns to reason and seeks answer to 'how and why' of everything scientifically.

This is also the age of specialization. By now aptitudes begin to show and the individual has developed his reasoning and stabilized his interests. He begins to conceive great ideals and aspires for doing something in life.

In India, we have a common curriculum with various subjects though we follow various streams like SSC, SSLC, ICSE, CBSE, matriculation etc. Work experience has been defined by the Education Commission (1964-66) as "Participation in productive work, in school, in the home, in a workshop, or a farm, or a factory, or in any other productive situation.

The introduction to the world of work is a career-education programme very well thought out, to help students to decide on their future plan of action, after undergoing a series of educational/vocational exercises. To make this programme a success, educational guidance is essential both for the teacher and the students, to collect and disseminate educational and career information and make a detailed study of themselves. The introduction of the World of Work Programme itself is a complete educational/guidance programme, through which proper guidance would be received by the school-leavers. If the student opts for any of the other branches, an administration of a battery of psychological tests would be needed to identify the potential and to find out whether the individual can opt for the same specific branch after school.

The most important task to achieve is to help the student to obtain the maximum grade in the School Leaving Certificate Examination. In this, the teachers and the parents need to see that each and every child is attended to and each one uses his/her capacity to the fullest. In a class of fifty or sixty, there will be different categories of students, like weak, average, good, very good and the gifted children. Majority will fall in the average category.

The weak students should be given special care through diagnostic and remedial instructions. This can be given through special coaching classes or by teaching the same topic again and again for them. If correctly motivated, they can surely reach the expected level.

DON'T QUIT !

When things go wrong, as they sometimes will,

When the road you're trudging seems all uphill,

When the funds are low and the debts are high,

And you want to smile, but you have to sigh,

When care is pressing you down a bit —

Rest if you must, but don't you quit.

Life is queer with its twists and turns

As every one of us sometimes learns,

And many a fellow turns about

When he might have won had he stuck it out.

Don't give up though the pace seems slow —

You may succeed with another blow.

Often the goal is nearer than

It seems to a faint and faltering man;

Often the struggler has given up

When he might have captured the victor's cup;

And he learned too late

When the night came down

How close he was to the golden crown.

Success is failure turned inside out —

The silver tint of the clouds of doubt,

And you never can tell how close you are,

It may be near when it seems a far,

So stick to the light when you're hardest hit —

It's when things seem worst that you mustn't quit.

Don't quit but turn to God !

While the average, good and very good students can reach their expected level through diagnostic and remedial instructions, motivation, and encouragement from the beginning itself there may be some underachievers in these categories. It is the ability and the interest of the teacher to identify these children and to find out the cause for their underachievement and take the necessary steps to bring them up to the expected level.

The gifted children should be given enrichment programmes which will include more challenging and intellectually stimulating activities.

Some of the activities are :

- Working on independent projects.
- Experimentation and independent research.
- Special assignments that can be from within the syllabus or from outside the syllabus.
- Construction of models and teaching aid materials.
- Preparing reports and participation in panel discussions.
- Independent library reading.
- Organising quiz programmes etc.,

These activities not only provide facilities for the full development of the special abilities and potentialities of the child but also care for the development of both the average and the gifted. Both the groups can develop according to their own abilities and capacities without interfering in the development of others.

There may be blockage or learning disabilities in some students. Some of the factors that contribute to learning difficulties are of a permanent kind while others are temporary in character and can be easily prevented or corrected. Some of the factors that contribute to learning disabilities are mental or intellectual factors, emotional factors, volitional factors and social and moral factors. (Refer - Late Childhood.)

These factors could have been identified earlier in late childhood and appropriate steps could have been taken to correct them or to prevent them. If these were found just at this stage or the diagnosis was neglected earlier, whatever the case may be, corrective and preventive measures should be taken immediately so that these students can be brought to their expected achievement level. Therefore, the immediate need over here is Remedial Teaching Programmes. (Refer - Late Childhood.)

The guidance counsellors motivate the school leavers to put their best efforts or else their onward journey would be jeopardized. Again the entire educational standard of the school is judged by the performance of these pupils at the external examination and therefore, the guidance counsellors play a very vital role in making sure that the best of the educational facilities are provided to the students.

The guidance counsellor's help is needed the most at this stage of education. As discussed earlier, since the teenagers are going through the adolescent stage, all problems of the adolescent stage come to the fore like clumsy physical growth, setting in of puberty and development of sex organs; emotional immaturity, showing great excitement or deep depression, amorality and undue religious fervours. The guidance counsellors would be the pivots round which all guidance programmes for students can be organized, career masters providing career information, subject teacher guiding them into specialized courses and programmes. Teachers conduct activities for the study of self and the librarian, keeping the new literature and information known to the students; office staff maintaining all records of pupils up-to-date, including cumulative record card, medical records and so on. If the counsellor organizes educational guidance programmes carefully with the help of all the personnel available in the school set up, the school leavers would not have to run from pillar to post for information as to what they should do after the 10th or 12th. Many times students move from one guidance agency to another or from one college to another not knowing what to do and where to go. The worse is the case of individuals who are not so good in their scholastic work and either desire to get into employment market as apprentices or take up short term vocational training courses.

Vocationalisation of education at the higher secondary stage can solve a number of educational problems.

Higher Secondary Stage: When the educational structure 10+2+3 was introduced, it was hoped that at the end of Std.X general education having terminated, 40% of the students would be bifurcated to short term vocational training courses and only 60% would pursue higher secondary academic courses. Educational guidance programmes, if faithfully followed could have led to such a situation but unfortunately this was not so. The society was not ready for the change, and all those who completed the Xth standard rushed to H.S.C. Science, Commerce and Arts respectively in the order of priority mentioned. Whatever good could have occured from the new structure was totally lost for the dream of vocationalising the + 2 stage namely the higher secondary only remained on paper.

Vocationalisation of Education: In the vocationalisation of education, the goal is to prepare children for a wide range of avenues in work life. The goal is not in meeting specific manpower planning needs but to orient pupils to a range of work areas in technical, commercial, paramedical, preprimary teaching, home management, agricultural and other areas; and to determine the range in response to local employment needs. However, with all said and done, there is a deep seated conviction that broad-based higher academic education is a passport to a respectable job that pupils should pass examinations and postpone vocational decisions till at a later date.

Our educational system must help our students to discover themselves to understand the components of their conscious and unconscious personalities, the mechanisms of brain, the operation of intelligence, the laws governing their physical development, the meaning of their dreams and aspirations and above all, the nature of their relations with one another and with the community at large. The task of educational institutions is not merely to seek out aptitudes, train them and give them a seal of approval. It must also develop personality and attitudes. **EDUCATION, TO BE WORTHWHILE SHOULD MAKE A MAN, ONE WHO IS ABLE AND A RESPONSIBLE MEMBER OF THE SOCIETY.**

LETTER TO THE PARENTS

Dear Parents,

I know that parents have that sound parental instincts and they have the potential to understand and manage the most complicated of situations and communications of your children. Most parents desperately want to do their best as parents and are bewildered, confused and hurt when in spite of doing their best things seem to go 'wrong'.

Parenting adolescents however, is a different kind of challenge. Not only are we sometimes unsure about what is best, we are dealing with teens who often have strong ideas of their own about what is best for them. There are many reasons why it is sometimes hard to know what is best for your teen. The world has changed drastically and teenagers are different today than just a generation ago. Traditional parenting roles have shifted as well.

Today's adolescents are different. While it is true that adolescents are different today but in other significant ways adolescents are the same as they have been for many years.

What makes it more difficult than ever to be an adolescent today is that the world they live in is less predictable than it was in the past. This makes the relationship between the parent and child much shakier, compared to a time when change happened more slowly.

Parenting has changed too. Three decades ago, children returned home to a parent, usually the mother, who stayed home full-time. Today both the parents are working and they are working for longer hours. Consequently, they are more stressed out and isolated and they don't even have the time to take care of their own emotional needs let alone the needs of their children.

Today many parents are less clear about what is important for them and what values and morals they want to pass on to their children. Sometimes parents say one thing and do another thereby sending unclear messages to their children.

Raising adolescents with love and understanding is more challenging than ever. Adolescence is a time of turmoil and turbulence of stress and storm. Rebellion against authority and against convention is to be expected and tolerated for the sake of learning and growth. It is not easy to watch a pleasant child turn into an unruly adolescent. There is also a sudden realization that "My child is no longer a child." This is a moment of elation and fear.

There is also conflict. As parents, our need is to be needed; as adolescents their need is not to need you. This conflict is real.

Children do not need perfect parents. What they do need is parents who are willing to understand what their behaviour is trying to communicate.

Therefore, accept their restlessness and discontent. It is the age of inconsistency and ambivalence.

One father says, "My 17-year-old is a handsome boy but he is an ugly girl. His long hair makes me mad. It is ridiculous to fight over it."

Wise parents know that fighting a teenager is inviting doom. So they flow with life.

Teenagers do not like their parents calling nicknames, or teasing them. They get insulted and get hurt deeply when it comes from parents. The damage may be permanent.

Do not treat your teenager like a child. Teenagers hate to be reminded of their babyhood. They want to distance themselves from childhood. They want to be considered grown ups. Do not show off your son's or daughter's nude photographs taken when he or she was just a baby.

The adolescent craves for independence and hates dependence. Therefore use statements that encourage independence. Like, "You make your decision." "The choice is yours." "Whatever you choose is fine with me." etc. etc.

Have healing dialogue with your adolescent. For example, if your son was hurt by someone's words or actions, do not look for the person's motives or to supply excuses for him. Your task is to show your son that you understood his anger, hurt and humiliation. The following statements may help your son as an emotional first aid.

"It must have been humiliating."

"It must have made you furious."

"It must have been hurting."

Or in other cases, like, to your daughter who told you that she was so tired.

"It has been such a long day for you." Or " You really look tired."

Teenagers need privacy. By providing privacy, respect is demonstrated. Once a boy complained "My mother has no respect for me. She checks my mail and wants to know who has sent the mail".

Do not label your children. Labelling is dangerous. Do not pass contradictory and confusing messages.

Acknowledge your children's experience instead of denying or arguing about his experience. For example, if your son says, "Oh, the coffee is too hot." Accept it as hot!

Use constructive and helpful criticism. It doesn't address itself to the personality. It deals with the situation, event or problem. It never attacks the person.

When Diana failed in Mathematics in the first semester, her father called her for a conversation and concentrated on one point: " What can be done to do better in this a difficult subject ?" Father did not blame or threaten anybody. He maintained a problem solving attitude.

Give your children positive and sincere praise. Give praise or credit for the work or the action. For example - Pat, wrote an essay. The teacher praised the essay and said, Pat, "Your essay was well written." Pat was encouraged to write essays again.

PARENTS NEED TO BE THE 'ROLE MODELS'

This is the greatest challenge before any parent. We are the source of our children's biological being. We are also the source of much of what they know about the world and how they view it. Our challenge is to be the kind of people that we want our sons and daughters to become.

If we want our children to be respectful, then we need to model respect.

If we want our children to be responsible, then we need to model responsible behaviour.

If we want our children to be truthful, then we need to model truthfulness.

If we want our children to admit their mistakes, then we need to admit our mistakes and apologize.

If we want our children to be faithful and loyal, then we need to model faithfulness and loyalty.

If we want our children to be forgiving, then we need to model forgivingness.

If we need our children to love and care, then we need to model love and care.

As you model these values and behaviour, you will discover your adolescents living out the same values and behaviour.

Your children want you to love each other and have a happy and peaceful life. Your children WISH THE BEST FOR YOU.

Teenagers need you both. They need your love and care through various actions of yours.

A boy of 16 shared with me how he misses both the parents care and how he wished if his parents were living together happily. His parents have been living separately for many years. His mother was very much affected by this and became aloof from the children though she was living with them. He wished his mother had served food for him when he had returned home after school. He wished if his parents were there for family meals.

The following is a small portion of his letter :

Name and Address
---

doesn't care,
such as giving food
et proper time

For Taking care after
field and all.
He doesn't come to meet
us
Whenever I tell father
to come and see us, he
doesn't come, just
looking after properly).
Ma hates him (papa).
Papa doesn't think of Ma
anymore

Within a year of this boy's confiding to me, the parents were reunited and the boy's grandfather was very happy to inform me about their happy reunion. Today this boy is a surgeon in one of Delhi's well-known hospitals.

Dear Parents, though parents are often at a loss as to how to relate to their adolescents, they nevertheless want to continue to be involved in their adolescents' lives. The heart of successful parenting of adolescents is the relationship that we form with them. Building a relationship of mutual respect, love and understanding and providing support and consistency are the foundations of effective parenting.

A TEACHER'S PRAYER

Give me, Divine Master,
a sincere love for my students,
and deep respect for each one's unique gifts.
Help me to be a faithful and devoted teacher,
with my eyes on the good of those I serve.
May I impart knowledge humbly
listen attentively,
collaborate willingly,
and seek the lasting good of those I teach.

     May I be quick to understand,
     slow to condemn,
     eager to affirm and to forgive.
     While I teach ideas and give training in skills,
     may my life and my integrity
     open minds and hearts to the truth.
     May my warm-hearted interest in each one
     give them a zest for life and a passion for learning.
     Give me the strength to admit my limitations.
     the courage to start each day with hope.
     and the patience and humour I need in my
     teaching.

I accept each student from Your hands.
I believe that everyone of them
is a person of unique worth,
even when they themselves do not see it.
I know that I have the opportunity
to bring light and hope.
a sense of mission and purpose
to many young lives
I believe that You believe in me,
and You stand by me.

     I seek Your blessing
     as I start another day.

I ask You to bless me and my students,
and our dreams and hopes.
May we learn from the wisdom of the past.
May we learn from life and from one another.

May we, above all,
learn from Your guidance
and from the lives of those who know You best.
For this is true learning :
to know life as it should be lived;
to know ourselves as we truly are,
and to hear Your voice in every word we learn.

— By Joe Mannath

A good teacher must know how to arouse the interest of the pupil in the field of study for which he is responsible; he must himself be a master in the field and be in touch with the latest developments in his subject; he must himself be a fellow traveller in the exciting pursuit of knowledge.

— Dr. S. Radhakrishnan

Bibliography

BOOKS

1. Elizabeth B.Hurlock : Developmental Psychology, A Lifespan Approach, Fifth edition, M/s Tata McGraw Hill Company Ltd. New Delhi.
   - (a) Prenatal stage. Some common physical hazards during the prenatal period. The effects of attitudes of significant people on children before and after birth. Some negative attitudes which will lead to psychological hazards during the prenatal period.
   - (b) Infancy. Eating habits, Sleep habits. The habits of elimination and emotional insecurity in Children.
   - (c) Early childhood. Ordinal position.Some factors that contribute to happiness in early childhood.
   - (d) Later childhood. Some behavioural disorders. Some learning difficulties.

2. S.K. Mangal : Educational Psychology, M/s Parkash Brothers, Ludhiana.
   - (a) The Stage of Childhood.
   - (b) Adolescence Stage & Special Characteristics of Adolescence

3. Dr. (Miss) Mehroo D. Bengalee. Guidance and Counselling, Second Edition. M/s Sheth Publishers Pvt. Ltd. Mumbai.
   - (a) Philosophy of Guidance
   - (b) The Assumptions
   - (c) The Goals to Achieve in Guidance
   - (d) The Stages of Development According to Biiehler
   - (e) The Need Established by Kothari Commission (1964–1966)
   - (f) Guidance and Counselling
   - (g) Need for Guidance in Modern Society
   - (h) Stages of Educational Guidance
     - (i) Pre-Primary Stage
     - (ii) Primary Stage
     - (iii) Upper Primary Stage
     - (iv) Secondary Stage
     - (v) Higher Secondary Stage.

4. Barbara Cartland, Sex and the Teenager. Published by M/s Pauline Publications. Mumbai
(*a*) Why you are Here ?

5. Dr. S.K. Mangal — 1986, Education Psychology, Prakash Brothers, Educational
Publishers, Books Market, Ludhiana **(Habit Formation in Children)**

6. Dr. S.K. Mangal — 1986, Education Psychology, Prakash Brothers, Educational
Publishers, Books Market, Ludhiana **(Mental Hygiene in Children, Why Does One
Forget?, Training in Memory)**

7. Dr. Mehroo D. Bengalee — 1976, Sheth Publishers, Educational Publishers, 35,
Everest, Peddar Rol, Mumbai - 400026. **(Exceptional Children)**

8. Dr. S.K. Mangal — 1986, Education Psychology, Prakash Brothers, Educational
Publishers, Books Market, Ludhiana. **(Exceptional Children)**